THE

Unseen Real

THE
Unseen Real

Life in the Light of the Ascension of Jesus

STEPHEN SEAMANDS

Scripture quotations, unless otherwise indicated, are from New Revised Standard Version Bible, copyright © 1989 National Council of the Churches of Christ in the United States of America. Used by permission. All rights reserved.

Scripture quotations marked NLT are taken from the Holy Bible, New Living Translation, copyright 1996. Used by permission of Tyndale House Publishers, Inc., Wheaton, Illinois 60189. All rights reserved.

Scripture quotations marked NIV are taken from the Holy Bible, New International Version®, NIV®. Copyright © 1973, 1978, 1984 by Biblica, Inc.™ Used by permission of Zondervan. All rights reserved worldwide. www.zondervan.com

Scripture quotations marked KJV are taken from the *Holy Bible*, King James Version, Cambridge, 1796.

Printed in the United States of America

Cover design by Strange Last Name
Page design by PerfecType, Nashville, Tennessee

Seamands, Stephen A., 1949-
The unseen real : life in the light of the ascension of Jesus / Stephen Seamands. – Frankin, Tennessee : Seedbed Publishing, ©2016.

141 pages ; 21 cm.

ISBN 9781628243550 (paperback : alk. paper)
ISBN 9781628243567 (Mobi)
ISBN 9781628243574 (ePub)
ISBN 9781628243581 (uPDF)

1. Christian Life--Methodist authors. 2. Conduct of life--Religious aspects--Christianity. 3. Bible. Colossians, III, 1-3--Criticism, interpretation, etc. 4. Jesus Christ--Ascension.   I. Title.

BV4501.3 .S4252 2016   248.4/876   2016949508

SEEDBED PUBLISHING
Franklin, Tennessee
seedbed.com

To all the students I have been blessed to teach at
Asbury Theological Seminary (1983–2017)

Contents

CHAPTER ONE

A Mind Set on Heaven

So if you have been raised with Christ, seek the
things that are above, where Christ is, seated at the
right hand of God. Set your minds on things that
are above, not on things that are on earth, for you
have died, and your life is hidden with Christ in God.

—COLOSSIANS 3:1–3

A s a young Christian I was often warned not to be
"so heavenly minded you're no earthly good." But
in the verses above, Paul urged the fledgling Colossian
believers to be *more* heavenly minded, not less.

"So if you have been raised with Christ," he instructed
them, "*seek* the things that are above" (Col. 3:1, italics
mine). The apostle wanted them to desire, pursue, and
run after heavenly things. He also told them to "set [their]
minds on things above," which implies thinking about,
reflecting upon, and contemplating heavenly things. The

New Living Translation captures it well: "Set your sights on the realities of heaven" (Col. 3:1 NLT).

Paul was not merely making a suggestion. In the original Greek, the verbs are in the imperative mood. That means he was giving a command. They are also in the *present* tense, which implies continuous ongoing action. Paul, then, was insisting that the Colossians *do* this, *keep on* doing it, and do it *always*. His concern was not that these young Christians would be *too* heavenly minded, but not heavenly minded *enough*. He wanted their earth to be crammed with heaven.

Not, however, so they would despise earthly things or withdraw from the world. Not in order to avoid present suffering by escaping into a pie-in-the-sky future. Suffice it to say, the heavenly mindedness Paul wanted them to seek after was for the sake of, not the denial of, the earth and the world. That's why he spent the rest of his letter telling the Colossians how they should conduct themselves in a wide range of practical, down-to-earth contexts and relationships (Col. 3:5–4:6). He discussed everything from personal morality, relationships in community, worship, marriage, parenting, work, time management, and relating to outsiders. Paul then urged them to focus on heavenly things so they could truly and rightly engage in earthly things.

The apostle believed—and so have wise Christians ever since—that if you want to properly love this present world, you must think about the next. Your heaven will determine your earth. So if you want to change earth, set your mind on heaven. As C. S. Lewis put it, "Aim at heaven and you will get earth 'thrown in.'" If you aim only at earth, "you will get neither."[1] For the sake of the earth, then, Paul wanted the Colossians to be more heavenly minded, not less.

Where Christ Is Seated at the Right Hand of God

He also wanted them to seek after and set their minds on the realities of heaven *for the sake of knowing Christ.* Because, according to Paul, heaven is "where Christ is, seated at the right hand of God" (Col. 3:1).

Now when we think about "where Christ is," most likely "seated at the right hand of God" is not what comes to mind. Paul told us to "set [our] minds on things that are above, *not on things that are on earth*" (Col. 3:2, italics mine). But when we think about Jesus, that's often the very thing we end up doing. We bring him down to our level and view him from the perspective of earth below, not of heaven above where, according to Paul, he is seated now.

As a result we think of Jesus either from the horizon of the past (what he accomplished on earth for us through his life, death, and resurrection) or from the horizon of the future (when he shall return to judge and to reign over the earth). And, of course, there's nothing wrong in doing that. In the New Testament he was often viewed from both of those horizons.

But this is incomplete. What's obviously missing is the horizon of the present—what Jesus, as the one who has ascended into heaven and sits at the right hand of God, is doing now. No wonder Paul urged us to seek after and set our minds upon things above. He wanted us to understand and encounter Jesus from the horizon of the present, from the perspective of today, not merely from the perspective of yesterday or someday.

And, by the way, today—the present—was the dominant horizon of the New Testament writers, the way they most often viewed Christ. If then we read the story of Jesus only or primarily from the horizon of the past or the future, we will inevitably misread and misinterpret it.

When we think of heaven, for example, we think primarily about the future. Heaven is the place you go after you die. In heaven you'll be with Jesus and the saints and your loved ones forever. There will be pearly gates and streets of gold, and no more crying, suffering, or pain. In heaven we will gather around the throne with people from every tongue and tribe and nation to worship and praise God forever. We can cite particular scriptures that describe all these things happening in the heaven of the future. And we should. Thank God for the blessed hope that we have!

But the "things above"—the heavenly realities Paul wanted us to seek after and set our minds on—are not primarily in the future yet to come. Instead, he wanted us to fix our gaze on the heaven that is *already* present, where Christ is ascended, seated, and reigning at God's right hand. We think of heaven as a place we go to after we die. For Paul and the writers of the New Testament, it was, above all, a dimension Christians inhabit *now*.

In biblical cosmology, as N. T. Wright explained, heaven and earth are not different locations, far apart from each other.[2] They are different dimensions of God's creation (Gen. 1:1). Heaven and earth can overlap and interlock with each other. They're not like oil and water that don't mix. In fact, because heaven relates to earth tangentially, it touches and permeates earth. So the poet, Elizabeth Barrett Browning, is right: Earth is "crammed with heaven."[3]

Though the original close, intimate connection between the two has been deeply ruptured by humanity's fall into sin and evil, God has been faithfully at work in a redemptive process slowly repairing the connection. Jesus' life, death, resurrection, and ascension are at the very heart and center of that process. In the end when Christ returns, the connection will be fully restored. The two will be joined together as God intends (Rev. 21–22). The last line of the hymn, "This Is My Father's World" sums it up well: "Jesus who died will be satisfied, and earth and heav'n be one."[4]

That is why Christ's ascension from earth to heaven is such a significant event. It further establishes and forges the connection, forever binding heaven and earth together. In the divine-human person of the ascended Christ, they have been and are now bound together eternally.

And that—we can't emphasize it enough—is the dominant horizon of the New Testament for viewing Jesus. Not from the horizon of the past or future, but from the horizon of the present, where the ascended Christ is sitting in heaven at God's right hand. The fact that *today* he is reigning as the ascended Lord both validates and vindicates his *yesterday* (Christ's life, death, and resurrection) and assures and guarantees his *tomorrow* (Christ's final return and victory).

When I am trying to get this across to a group of pastors and Christian leaders, I often start by asking them a question: What Old Testament verse is either directly quoted or alluded to in the New Testament more than any other? The vast majority don't know. You should see the puzzled looks on their faces. Most are hesitant to even venture a guess.

So I say, "Let me help you. Is it (A) Psalm 23:1: 'The LORD is my shepherd, I shall not want'; (B) Leviticus 11:45: 'You shall be holy, for I am holy'; (C) Isaiah 53:5: 'He was wounded for our transgressions, crushed for our iniquities'; or (D) Deuteronomy 6:5: 'You shall love the LORD your God with all your heart, and with all your soul, and with all your might'"? Most of them lean toward D. Since it is the Great Commandment, it would seem the logical choice.

But then I smile and say, "Actually, it's none of the above!" They usually laugh and protest. Then I give them the correct answer. It's Psalm 110:1: "The LORD says to my lord: 'Sit at my right hand until I make your enemies a footstool for your feet" (NIV). And that verse, I inform them, is either directly quoted or alluded to in the New Testament a total of twenty times.[5]

Now they are even more puzzled and surprised! Why that verse? It's certainly not the verse we would have picked! What is it about that verse that caused the New Testament writers to keep coming back to it?

The Significance of Psalm 110:1

You may recall that before there was an Apostles' Creed, the earliest Christian confession was simply, "Jesus is Lord!" When the early Christians said that, they were declaring that Jesus, the one who had been rejected and crucified, had been raised from the dead. But not only had God raised him from the dead, Jesus had also been exalted to God's right hand and enthroned as Lord and King.

The foremost reason, then, that they kept citing Psalm 110:1 was because it underscored the fact that Jesus is Lord. Devout Jews at the time of Christ believed this verse, along with the entire psalm, referred not only to Israel's past Davidic kings, but also to the future Messiah who was to come. Convinced Jesus was that Messiah, the early Christians therefore boldly applied it directly to him. Peter, in fact, declared it in the sermon he preached to the crowd gathered on the day of Pentecost. After his earthly ministry, he proclaimed Messiah Jesus, Son of God and Risen Lord, ascended and returned to his Lord and Father in heaven, who said to him, "Sit at my right hand, until I make all your enemies your footstool." God, therefore, has made this Jesus, whom you crucified, "both Lord and Messiah" (Acts 2:32–36).

The New Testament writers, therefore, kept returning to Psalm 110:1 in order to proclaim the resurrected Christ's exaltation to the place of honor at God's right hand and his installation and enthronement as Messiah and King. As the writer of Hebrews put it, alluding to this verse, "When he had made purification for sins, he sat down at the right hand of the Majesty on high" (Heb. 1:3). His time of humiliation and death was over, so too were his resurrection appearances. His earthly ministry was complete; now his heavenly ministry had begun.

Paul magnificently summed it up in the beginning of his letter to the Ephesians. God displayed his great power in Christ "when he raised him from the dead and seated him at his right hand in the heavenly places, far above all rule and authority and power and dominion. . . . And he has put all things under his feet and has made him the head over all things for the church, which is his body, the fullness of him who fills all in all" (Eph. 1:20–23).

For the New Testament writers, Psalm 110:1 was foundational in understanding who Jesus is and fully and properly exalting him. He is not only risen but reigning, not only alive but sovereign, not only central but supreme. All things—in the world, politics, society, history, culture, their personal lives—were to be viewed from the vantage point of the ascended Christ, "who has gone into heaven and is at the right hand of God, with angels, authorities, and powers made subject to him" (1 Peter 3:22). That was the horizon that shaped and determined everything else. Instead of relegating him to the past or the future, it situated him in the present and the center.

Opening Our Eyes That We Might See

The ascension, then, "where Christ is seated at the right hand of God" (Col. 3:1), is the dominant horizon of the New Testament. But it is definitely *not* the horizon from which we usually view things. That's why Paul reminded us to seek after and set our minds there. We are so prone to forget! Our natural tendency is to do the exact opposite of what Paul told us—to set our minds on things that are on earth, not on things above, and then to view Jesus from that perspective. Because of the universal nature of human sinfulness and brokenness (Rom. 3:9–20; Eph. 2:1–3), I believe this is true for all people everywhere. We set our minds on earthly things.

But it has become especially true for those of us in Western culture. For the past three hundred years, since the Age of the Enlightenment, we've been told that the *only* things that are real are the things of earth, those things we can perceive with our five senses. So if you can't see, hear, smell, taste, or touch it, you may personally think it's real, but you can't be sure, nor can you insist it must be real for anyone else.

One hundred years ago, G. K. Chesterton explained what has happened in modern Western culture like this:[6] When the wind is blowing and the branches of the trees are waving, there are two kinds of people in the world. One group believes the wind moves the branches; the other group believes the motion of the trees creates the wind. For most of human history and in most parts of the world today, people adhere to the former view. The consensus has been that the invisible lies behind and is the source of the visible. Only recently, and particularly in the West, has the latter view emerged, that the motion of the trees creates the wind.

Unfortunately this recent view has had a profound and pervasive influence on Western culture. As a result, belief in the *unseen real* is no longer a part of the average person's plausibility structure. It has also profoundly influenced and shaped Western Christianity, turning most of us into practical, functional deists, depriving us of spiritual imagination, and diminishing our capacity for contemplation.[7]

This Western worldview, of course, directly contradicts and is antithetical to the biblical worldview, where what is real simply cannot be reduced to what is empirically verifiable. In addition to the *seen* real, the Bible assumes and affirms the reality of the *unseen* real. In fact, the unseen real is considered more real, more ultimate than the seen real. As Fred Rogers (the famous Mr. Rogers) often said in quoting from *The Little Prince* (21:36), "What is essential is invisible to the eye."[8]

As I write this I am in my office in my home in Wilmore, Kentucky, where I have lived for many years. So if you were to ask me where I am sitting right now, I would say, "I'm in my office at home, sitting on a large comfortable swivel-back chair; in front of the desk where my laptop is turned on." And no doubt, what I've just told you is true. It's real—I'm not imagining it. I'm not in some sort of Matrix right now!

But, as we've noted, according to the New Testament, because I am "in Christ" I'm also sitting somewhere else. Paul said, I have been "raised with Christ" (Col. 3:1) and am seated "with him in the heavenly places" (Eph. 2:6). That means I'm seated "here" in my office, but I'm also seated "there" in the heavenly places. Both are true and real. But which of the two seatings is more real and more ultimate? This one (on my office chair) or that one (enthroned with Christ in heaven)? This one may appear to be more real—I can see and touch and feel the chair in my office. But the truth is, it will soon pass away. It won't be long before I'm not living here anymore! That one (enthroned with Christ), however, is an eternal seating and will never pass away.

According to Scripture, then, there is more to reality than the seen real. In fact, the unseen real is actually more real, more ultimate than the seen real. That's what Elisha the prophet had to get his servant to realize (see 2 Kings 6:11–23). They were staying in the city of Dothan at the time, and when the king of Aram (Syria) found out Elisha was there, he sent his soldiers to capture him.

Elisha had been helping his archenemy, the king of Israel, elude his attacks so the king of Aram wanted Elisha dead.

The king's soldiers came in the darkness of night and surrounded the city. The next morning when Elisha's servant looked out and saw them with their horses and chariots, he trembled. "What are we going to do now!" he cried out to Elisha.

But Elisha didn't seem the least bit concerned. "Do not be afraid," he told his servant, *"There are more with us than there are with them"* (2 Kings 6:16, italics mine).

I doubt the servant found Elisha's words particularly reassuring. I can imagine him thinking to himself, "Yeah, right!" So Elisha prayed, "O LORD, please open his eyes that he may see" (2 Kings 6:17).

And the Scripture says, "So the LORD opened the eyes of the servant, and he saw; the mountain was full of horses and chariots of fire all around Elisha" (2 Kings 6:17).

For Elisha there was the seen real, but there was also an unseen real, and that made all the difference! Too often, however, like Elisha's servant, we view things only from the perspective of the seen real. We set our minds on things below, not things above. We, too, need to have our eyes opened to see and grasp the reality of the unseen real.

It's fascinating how, as the story continued to unfold, that perspective shaped what Elisha did. He prayed and God temporarily blinded the soldiers who were surrounding the city. Then he led the blinded soldiers to the king of Israel!

Naturally, the king wanted to kill them—they were his enemies. But Elisha said, "How can you do that? You didn't capture them. Give them food and water instead. Then send them back to their master." I'm sure the king of Israel was bewildered at that suggestion. But he did what the prophet said. In fact, he went further, and "prepared for them a great feast." Then, "after they ate and drank, he sent them on their way, and they went to their master" (2 Kings 6:23).

What a strange military strategy that was! It reminds me of Paul's exhortation: "If your enemies are hungry, feed them; if they are thirsty, give them something to drink" (Rom. 12:20). But here's the point: because Elisha "saw" and recognized the unseen real, he battled in a different way, "waging war," as Paul put it, not according to human standards but with divine power (2 Cor. 10:3–4).

And amazingly, it worked! When his soldiers returned and told him what had happened, the king of Aram was discombobulated. "Why in the world would my enemy prepare a feast for my soldiers? He feeds them better than I do! He must not be afraid of me? What kind of god does he have protecting him? I better leave him alone." Those might have been some of his thoughts. But we do know how the story ends: "And the Arameans no longer came raiding into the land of Israel" (2 Kings 6:23).

Too often, like Elisha's servant, we view things only from the perspective of the seen real. And that not only fuels our fears, it shapes how we work to overcome situations, circumstances, and persons who threaten us. We rely upon human wisdom, skill, and strength. We fight power with power, waging war according to human standards. We set our minds on things below, not things above.

What a difference it can make when our eyes are opened so that we may see. Oswald Chambers described it like this: "Suppose Jesus suddenly lifted the veil from our eyes and let us see angels ministering to us, His own presence with us, the Holy Spirit in us, and the Father around us—how amazed we should be! We have lived in the muddle of things instead of in the middle of things. Faith gets us into the middle, which is God and God's purpose."[9]

By Faith and Not by Sight

How true! When we reduce reality to the seen real, we live in the muddle of things. And Chambers was right: "faith gets us into the middle." These heavenly realities, "where Christ is seated at the right hand of God" (Col. 3:1) and we are "seated with him in the heavenly places" (Eph. 2:6), are dimensions of the unseen, not the seen real. Faith is the spiritual sense that enables us to perceive and grasp the reality of the unseen real.

In fact, according to the oft-quoted definition of faith in Hebrews 11, that's what faith is: "the assurance of things hoped for, the conviction of things *not seen*" (Heb. 11:1, italics mine). As Gordon Smith put it,

"Nothing so marks faith as this: that a person recognizes and lives in the reality that there is another order to life beyond what we can engage with our five senses."[10]

So we live in this seated with Christ position by faith and not by sight. As Charles Wesley expressed in one of his ascension hymns:

By faith already there,
In thee our Head we are
With our great forerunner we
Now in heavenly places sit,
Banquet with the Deity,
See the world beneath our feet.[11]

If, then, "where Christ is seated at the right hand of God" is to be the horizon from which we view things, a growing, deepening active faith is indispensable. For our earth to be crammed with heaven, nothing is more crucial.

Yet we know, based on our many failures and experiences, that nothing is so fragile, weak, and unstable in our lives as our faith. Frustrating circumstances, external pressures and opposition, internal fears, the constant stress of the daily grind, our preoccupation with the cares of this world—all combine to challenge and deplete our faith. How quickly we forget that we are seated with Christ and our lives are hid with Christ in God. The disconnect between what we *believe is true* and what we *experience as real* fuels doubt and fear and causes unbelief to rise.

If faith is to continue, deepen, grow, and increase in us, if we are to live by faith and not by sight, we must ever be determined and disciplined in nurturing, cultivating, and exercising it. Paul, as we've already noted, didn't merely suggest, but commanded us to seek after and set our minds on things above. When we are intentional about doing that, then we put ourselves in a place where God can impart to us the assurance of that reality. Faith in the reality of heaven, which we have affirmed and sought by exercising our wills, can then rise in us as the divinely given "conviction of things not seen." What we believe to be true and experience as real will then become one.

Living an Ascension-Shaped Life

In the chapters that follow, as we seek after and set our minds on things above, we will be focusing upon Paul's words, "where Christ is, seated at the right hand of God" (Col. 3:1). As we reflect and meditate on them, we will essentially be considering the meaning and significance of Christ's ascension for us.

"He ascended into heaven and sits at the right hand of God the Father Almighty" is a central tenet of the Christian faith and affirmed in all the major historic Christian creeds. However, it is one of the most neglected of all Christian beliefs, especially among Protestant Christians. Most of us have never heard someone preach or teach about it.

Sadly, some church leaders, having been shaped by the Western worldview and modern secularism, seem almost embarrassed by the ascension. Others merge it so closely with the resurrection of Christ that it loses its distinctive significance. Still others consider it too mystical or elevated to have any practical value for the ordinary Christian. I am convinced, however, that the ascension is an extremely important Christian belief and has enormous practical significance for our daily lives.

About twenty-five years ago, as I slowly worked through *The Holiest of All,* Andrew Murray's classic devotional commentary on Hebrews, I first began to grasp the significance of Christ's ascension and the reality of living an ascension-shaped life. No other New Testament book focuses on the ascension as much as Hebrews. Some scholars even suggest the entire book is actually an extended sermon on Psalm 110:1. In his commentary, Murray wrote this: "The knowledge of Jesus as having entered heaven for us, and taken us into union with himself into a heavenly life is what will deliver the Christian from all that is low and feeble, and lift [us] into a life of joy and strength."[12]

Convinced that he was right, I began to study and reflect, meditate, and pray about the meaning and significance of Christ's ascension. I came to realize how important it was to the early Christians and how, as I mentioned earlier, it was the dominant horizon from which the New Testament writers viewed Christ, themselves, and the world.

"Christ ascended to the right hand of God," said A. B. Simpson, "that he might lift us up into an ascension life."[13] In the chapters that follow, then, I want to unpack the meaning and significance of our belief in the ascension and what it means for us to live an ascension-shaped life. We will consider what the ascension means for Jesus and what it therefore means for us, i.e., for faith and practice in our ordinary lives as Christians. In each chapter, I will consider one key element of the doctrine and draw out some of its practical implications for us. At the end of the chapter, I will also include some questions that can be used for both personal and group reflection.

My prayer is that what follows will help you as you strive to follow Paul's instructions to seek after and set your mind on things above. That's where Christ is, seated at the right hand of God, and where you are, as a believer in Christ seated in the heavenly places with him. I pray that it will both deepen your faith and cause faith to rise in you, so that you may live a life on earth that is crammed with heaven.

Let me conclude this opening chapter with these inspiring words from Charles Haddon Spurgeon:

> It is sweet to remember that the exaltation of Christ in heaven is a *representative exaltation*. . . . His exaltation is *our* exaltation. He will give us to sit upon His throne, even as He has overcome, and is set down with His Father on His throne. . . . He has a throne, but He is not content with having a throne to Himself . . . He cannot

be glorified without His bride. Look up, believer, to Jesus now. . . . We have Christ for our glorious representative in heaven's courts now . . .[14]

Questions for Personal and Group Reflection

1. The New Testament Christians viewed everything from the perspective of the ascension of Christ. Why do you think the ascension is such a neglected topic among most Christians today?

2. Have you ever heard a sermon or a teaching on Christ's ascension? Does your church do anything to underscore its importance? What might your church do to emphasize it more?

3. Have you had moments where you have experienced "the reality of the *unseen* real"? What do you remember about those times? What long-term impact did they have on you?

4. Paul commanded us to "set our minds on things above, where Christ is seated at the right hand of God" (Col. 3:1ff). What are some of the reasons why this is difficult for you?

5. "Now we in heavenly places sit," wrote Charles Wesley in the hymn in this chapter. Then he immediately described in wonderful poetic imagery what that means: "Banquet with the Deity, See the world beneath our feet." Can you imagine yourself doing that? What might it look like?

CHAPTER TWO

The Now and Forever King

Lift up your heads, O gates!
and be lifted up, O ancient doors!
that the King of glory may come in.
Who is the King of glory?
The LORD, strong and mighty,
the LORD, mighty in battle. . . .
Who is this King of glory?
The LORD of hosts,
he is the King of glory.

—PSALM 24:7–10

Very few kings and queens are left in the world today, and they certainly don't rule with power and authority the way they once did. Take the British monarchy, for example. People all over the world are fascinated and intrigued by the grandeur, ceremony, and history associated with the royal family. Yet everyone knows their royalty is about style, not substance.

Granted, the king or queen is officially the head of state and the people of Britain are considered subjects, not citizens. But because England is a constitutional monarchy, the executive power of the monarch is strictly limited by constitutional rules. In practice, kings or queens are not allowed to exercise real political authority and must remain politically neutral. Their role then is largely symbolic—they represent Britain on state visits and ceremonial occasions, and serve as symbols of national unity.

The early Christians believed that when Jesus ascended into heaven he had been installed and exalted as King. Unlike a contemporary British monarch, however, his authority and power was much more than symbolic. Nor would his rule only begin when he returned to earth. Even now, they strongly insisted, Jesus is sitting at God's right hand, reigning as King and Lord of all.

To underscore his kingship, they often cited Psalm 110:1: "The LORD says to my lord: 'Sit at my right hand until I make all your enemies a footstool for your feet'" (NIV). According to Old Testament scholar James Luther Mays, when it was originally written, this verse and the entire psalm originally "served as a text for the installation of a king in office." During the time of Israel's kings, however, the office was far more than ceremonial or symbolic. As Mays explained, "The office was far more than a position; it was a status in the very order of things that endowed a person with identity and powers."[1] That's exactly how the early Christians understood the ascended

Christ's kingly office when they quoted Psalm 110:1. His kingship was real, powerful, and ultimate.

King over All

Here's why it's important to understand this. Looking around the world today with so much evidence to the contrary, we may be tempted to think that at present, like the current British monarch, Christ's kingship is only symbolic. With sin and suffering, pain and broken-ness, evil and injustice all around, how dare we proclaim that Jesus is reigning now? So it's easy to push his king-ship off into the future. "He's not *really* king now," we conclude, "But, of course, he will *become* king when he returns in the future."

So let me be clear and emphatic. When the early Christians confessed the ascended Christ is king, they weren't merely affirming what would only be true some-time in the distant future. As N. T. Wright stressed, the New Testament writers, "all think that Jesus is already in charge of the world. . . . That is what they understood by 'God's kingdom.'"[2] By proclaiming that he had ascended into heaven and is sitting at the right hand of God, they were announcing he was already King *now*.

Let me explain. Throughout the Bible, heaven is described as God's throne, the place from which God rules the world. As the psalmist declared, "The LORD has made the heavens his throne; from there he rules over everything" (Ps. 103:19 NLT; see also Pss. 93; 99:1; 123:1;

Isa. 66:1–2). Proclaiming then that Jesus has ascended *into heaven* means he is ruling over the world too. As New Testament scholar Richard Bauckham explained, "Jesus' exaltation was understood as his sharing the divine throne in heaven and thus participating in the divine rule over the cosmos."[3] That's why, in a number of places, New Testament writers explicitly describe the risen, ascended Christ as sitting on the Father's throne, reigning with God *now* (see Heb. 8:1; 12:2; Rev. 3:21; 5:6; 7:17; 22:3).

The fact that Jesus *sits* at God's right hand also underscores this. To this point, everything we have affirmed in the Apostles' Creed about "Jesus Christ, his only Son, our Lord," is in the past tense. He was conceived . . . born . . . suffered . . . died . . . crucified . . . buried . . . rose . . . ascended. But then suddenly, as Karl Barth pointed out, there is a *present* in the Creed.[4] Jesus *sits* at the Father's right hand. And, according to Kevin Vanhoozer, this means that in the unfolding drama of the Christian story, "the climax has been reached: all the other events pertaining to Jesus lie in the past, but his ruling from on high is present and ongoing."[5]

Christ's sitting as King at God's right hand (theologians call it his *session* or rule) is therefore the climax of the Christian story. What follows is merely the culmination, the unfolding and outworking of his reign. When he comes in the future he comes not to finally be *crowned and made* King, as if until then his kingship is in doubt or up for grabs! No. The fact that he is presently sitting at God's right hand means he *already* is King.

Jesus is reigning now! Most people in the world may be completely unaware of it. Some stubbornly refuse to acknowledge or submit to his rule; others actively rebel and work to undermine it. Christians who worship Christ the King are painfully aware of their ongoing resistance and rebellion. But it shouldn't cause them to think of his reign now as only partial or potential—as if his reign only becomes real when Jesus returns in the future.

Remember, there is *both* a seen and an unseen real. So we shouldn't reduce the reality of his reign to the seen real. Nor should we assume that the seen real is more real than the unseen real. Because something cannot be perceived by our five senses doesn't mean it's unreal or less real than something that can be perceived by them.

When Christ returns, what is *already* real—Jesus is Lord and King—will be perceived and evident to all—every eye will see him (Rev. 1:7). Then he who is now King will be recognized and acknowledged and affirmed as King by all. Every knee will bow and every tongue confess that Jesus Christ is Lord (Phil. 2:10–11). What is now the unseen real (in heaven) will become the seen real (on earth). What we see now only with spiritual eyes, we will then also see with our natural eyes. Faith will become sight.

For Christians, however, even now our "citizenship is in heaven" (Phil. 3:20). So we pray, "Let your kingdom come, on earth as it is in heaven" (Matt. 6:10). And we passionately seek after and purposely set our minds on things above where Christ the King now is, seated at

God's right hand. We strive to let the unseen real (things above) shape and define reality rather the seen real (things below). We want what we *believe* to determine what we *see*, instead of letting what we *see* determine what we *believe*. We purpose and strive to walk by faith, not by sight (Heb. 11:1).

Does this mean we are oblivious to suffering and evil? Or refuse to face the brokenness around us? Of course not. But we are called to look at everything—no matter how painful and perplexing it might be—from the vantage point of the ascended Christ and therefore the conviction that regardless of what we see, Christ is reigning now. In the words of the hymn writer:

This is my Father's world, O let me ne'er forget
That though the wrong seems oft so strong, God
is the Ruler yet.[6]

In light of the ascension, the New Testament writers declared Jesus is reigning as King now, in the present—not someday, but *today*. For them, "ascension language is sovereignty language."[7] In the face of hardship, opposition, and persecution, they refused to relegate Christ's kingship to the distant future. Neither should we.

Nor should we relegate his kingdom to a private sphere where Jesus is only a spiritual King who reigns in our hearts. In this view of things, by his ascension he escaped to heaven so he could be safe from his enemies on earth. He reigns in heaven now and believers join him by going there when they die. But here on earth he reigns only in the private and *not* the public sphere.

Wrong. That will never do! As we sing in "Rejoice, the Lord Is King!" Charles Wesley's great ascension hymn: "His kingdom shall not fail. *He rules o'er earth and heaven. The keys of death and hell are to our Jesus given.*"[8] Christ's ascension and enthronement crowns him as King over *all* now and forever. It is therefore a great *public* act. So we are to declare among the nations that "the LORD is king!" (Ps. 96:10).

As such—and the early Christians understood this well—Christ's ascension challenges and threatens every political structure of this world. Like it or not, Caesars and czars, presidents and prime ministers—are all now subject to King Jesus. Regardless of what they do—they may refuse, reject, rebel, and rail against his kingship—he is King forever and Lord of all.

The church is called to herald and proclaim this *public* reality—the enthronement and reign of Jesus— in every nation. Because he is seated at God's right hand, the early Christians believed that what had been described in Psalm 2 (another royal, messianic psalm like Psalm 110) had come to pass (cf. Acts 4:23–31). God had now "set [his] king on Zion, [his] holy hill." He had declared to Jesus, "You are my son; today I have begotten you" and "Ask of me, and I will make the nations your heritage, and the ends of the earth your possession." The kings and the rulers of the earth had also been given an ultimatum: "Serve the LORD with fear, with trembling kiss his feet, or he will be angry, and you will perish in the way" (Ps. 2:6–11).

The fact that Jesus is sitting at God's right hand means that he is King of all nations and his rule encompasses all things. As Paul triumphantly declared, "Therefore God also highly exalted him . . . so that at the name of Jesus every knee should bend, in heaven and on earth and under the earth" (Phil. 2:9–10). Christ has been enthroned "far above all rule and authority and power and dominion, and above every name that is named . . . And [God] has put all things under his feet and has made him the head over all things" (Eph. 1:21–22).

His kingship therefore, extends over *every* sphere of creation, knee and tongue, height and depth. No cosmic, global, societal, communal, or personal space lies outside it. He is Lord *of* all and King *over* all, period. In Abraham Kuyper's memorable words, "There is not one square inch of the entire creation about which Jesus Christ does not cry out, 'This is mine! This belongs to me!'"[9]

Of course, what we *see* at present is a far cry from that day when every knee and tongue in heaven and on earth finally submits to his claim. As the writer of the Hebrews said, "Yet at present we do not see everything subject to them" (Heb. 2:8 NIV). All his enemies are not a footstool for his feet. During this present stage of his rule, Christ is slowly working his redemptive purposes out across the face of the earth. And though he restrains evil to serve his purposes, he still permits evil to exist in ways difficult to fathom.

A humble, patient King, Jesus is not in a hurry because he wants "all to come to repentance" (2 Peter 3:9). He also reigns without violating or overriding human free will, which he himself has ordained. So we do not see all things subject to him now. Heartache and injustice, suffering and pain, opposition and persecution, still exist in the world.

"But" the writer of Hebrews immediately added, "we do see Jesus, who for a little while was made lower than the angels, *now crowned with glory and honor* because of the suffering of death . . ." (Heb. 2:9, italics mine). Though we don't see all things subject to him now (the *seen* real), nonetheless, Jesus is "crowned with glory and honor" (the *unseen* real). According to biblical commentator Luke Timothy Johnson, that means he has been enthroned at God's right hand and is reigning as king.[10]

The apostle Paul believed his kingship would pass through a series of phases before it is fully consummated and he "hands over the kingdom to God the Father" (1 Cor. 15:23-24). Yet now, in the midst of this world, Jesus Christ is "crowned with glory and honor," seated at the Father's right hand, reigning as Lord and King. Consequently, as Thomas Oden maintained, even "when we cannot see his kingdom reigning, we can still behold his glory and participate in the promise of his kingdom, quietly growing like a tiny mustard seed or yeast in bread."[11]

Dimensions of His Reign

Ascended into heaven and sitting at God's right hand, Jesus is now enthroned as King. As we seek, then, to draw out some of the practical implications of his reign, let's briefly consider some particular ways his kingship applies to each of those four spheres.

1. Personal

Enthroned over the Floods. Psalm 93 begins with a confident voice declaring: "The LORD is king, he is robed in majesty . . . He has established the world; it shall never be moved; your throne is established from of old" (Ps. 93:1–2). Yet the psalmist seems also profoundly aware of the threatening forces around him contradicting what he's just said. Yes, the Lord is King, but his world is chaotic and out of control. So he fearfully cries out: "The floods have lifted up, O LORD, the floods have lifted up their voice; the floods lift up their roaring" (Ps. 93:3).

A confident voice, a fearful voice—all in the span of three verses! Which one will prevail? The voice that expresses what he proclaims as *true*—the Lord reigns—or the voice expressing what he is experiencing as real—"The floods have lifted up"? The next verse tells us: "More majestic than the thunders of mighty waters, more majestic than the waves of the sea, majestic on high is the LORD!" (Ps. 93:4). In the midst of the floods, declares the psalmist, the Lord rules as King.

The challenge for us, likewise, especially when the floods are swirling all around us, is to declare that the Lord is King. That was what Paul was telling us to do when he commanded us to set our minds on things above, where the enthroned Christ is seated at the right hand of God. We need to get in the habit of affirming it throughout each day. In the words of another psalm, "The LORD sits enthroned over the flood; the LORD sits enthroned as king forever" (Ps. 29:10). Do you need to stop and repeat those words in relation to your life right now?

Who Is Our King? Are there areas of our lives where we are bowing down to other kings even as we proclaim Christ is King? Have we submitted to Jesus and made him Lord and King over all? Where are we still sitting on the throne? In which areas of our lives are we still insisting on being in control? Like the Israelites did so often, are we worshipping and serving both the Lord God and other gods? Remember Joshua and Elijah's challenge to the people to choose whom they would serve (see Joshua 24:15; 1 Kings 18:21).

Often we won't submit because we are afraid of the King. Like Adam and Eve, we've believed the serpent's lie that God wants to rule over us in order to dominate, oppress, and enslave us. We may have had parents, spouses, or other authority figures who have ruled over us like that, but Christ the King—remember he is the *Lamb* who sits on the throne (Rev. 7:17)—has no such desire or intentions. He is a wise, gentle, and gracious King. True to what the prophet Isaiah said, his throne will be established and upheld "with justice and with righteousness" (Isa. 9:7; cf. Psalm 72).

Remember in C. S. Lewis's *The Lion, the Witch and the Wardrobe,* when Lucy anxiously asked Mr. and Mrs. Beaver if Aslan, the lion she had been hearing so much about, but hadn't met yet, is *safe?* Mr. Beaver responded, "Who said anything about safe? 'Course he isn't safe. But he's good. He's the King, I tell you."

He's not *safe,* but he's *good.* What a wonderful description of Jesus. That's why it often gets quoted. But don't stop there. Mr. Beaver goes on to tells us why: "He's the King, I tell you."[12]

The truth is—as strange as it may seem—wherever Christ rules, whenever the government is on his shoulder (Isa. 9:6 KJV), the more we humans flourish and find fulfillment and freedom. So the worshippers around the throne cry out in jubilation, "You have made them to be a kingdom and priests serving our God, *and they will reign on earth*" (Rev. 5:10, italics mine). Where Christ reigns as King, we reign too! A couple of verses from George Matheson's hymn wonderfully convey the paradox:

> Make me a captive, Lord, and then I shall be free.
> Force me to render up my sword and I shall
>   conqueror be.
> I sink in life's alarms when by myself I stand;
> Imprison me within thine arms, and strong shall
>   be my hand. . . .

My will is not my own till thou has made it thine;
If it would reach a monarch's throne, it must its
   crown resign.
It only stands unbent amid the clashing strife,
When on thy bosom it has leant, and found in
   thee its life.[13]

Have you experienced that to be true in your life? Where in your life do you need to surrender and crown him King in order to flourish more, reign more, and enjoy more freedom?

2. Communal

It is interesting how in Ephesians, Paul linked Christ's ascension and enthronement as King with the church. God "raised him from the dead and seated him at his right hand in the heavenly places," Paul declared. And then he added, "He has put all things under his feet and has made him the head over all things *for the church,* which is his body" (Eph. 1:20–23, italics mine).

Often local churches forget who the rightful King and head of their church is. Sometimes pastors or prominent members and families act like they are! Much more could be said about that! Later in Ephesians, he did speak of Christ's kingship along these lines—of his being head *in* the church, and the church being subject to him (Eph. 5:22–24). But notice that here he said all things are under his dominion, not *in* the church but *for* the church.

So what did Paul mean? Since he didn't explain, we can't be absolutely sure. However, I think in his

Institutes of the Christian Religion, John Calvin, in his discussion of Christ's present reign as King, pointed us in the right direction. Despite the plots and efforts of his enemies, Calvin said that Christ the King presently rules over them all in protecting, defending, and preserving the church. "Hence, amid the violent agitation with which it is continually troubled, amid the grievous and frightful storms that threaten it with unbridled calamities, it still remains safe."[14] Calvin then quoted Psalm 110:1, which proves that no matter how many strong enemies plot to overthrow the church, "they do not have sufficient strength to prevail over God's immutable decree by which he appointed his Son eternal King."[15]

Being certain of this ought to renew our confidence, fill us with hope, and enable us to persevere through fiery trials and tribulations. As Calvin eloquently concluded, "Thus it is that we may patiently pass through this life with its misery, hunger, cold, contempt, reproaches, and other troubles—content with this one thing: that *our King will never leave us destitute,* but will provide for our needs until, our warfare ended, we are called to triumph. Such is the nature of his rule that he shares with us all that he has received from the Father. Now he arms and equips us with his power, adorns us with his beauty and magnificence, enriches us with his wealth" (italics mine).[16]

You don't have to be a Calvinist to say a hearty Amen to that! As King *for* the church, Christ defends and sustains her. As King, he arms, adorns, and enriches her.

Remember his promise: "I will build my church; and the gates of hell shall not prevail against it" (Matt. 16:18 KJV).

3. Social

Herod and Pilate understood well that calling Jesus King had profound social and political ramifications (Matt. 2:3; John 18:33). So did the Roman Caesars when the early Christians confessed that the risen, ascended Christ is Lord and King. It meant that Caesar wasn't! As the angry mob cried out, in trying to persuade Pilate to crucify Jesus, "Everyone who claims to be a king sets himself against the emperor" (John 19:12). Yet even when it meant death for them, the early Christians would not stop confessing it.

So how should our awareness that Jesus is King shape our approach to politics? In his insightful book *To Change the World*, James Davison Hunter analyzed the three major approaches among American Christians today—the Christian Right, the Christian Left, and the "neo-Anabaptists."[17] On the surface, they stand in stark contrast to each other, but actually all three share common assumptions. All three, Hunter observed, operate with a narrow, truncated view of power, conceiving of it primarily in political terms. Real power, it seems, is political power.

Furthermore, all three are driven primarily by something negative—what they are against—rather than something positive—what they are for. The Christian right fights against secular humanism; the Christian left fights against economic injustice (and the Christian right!); and the neo-Anabaptists fight against capitalism and the Constantinian state. As a result, Hunter maintained, they have become captive to *ressentiment*, the term the philosopher Friedrich Nietzsche coined from a French word for the rehearsal of grievances, to refer to a political psychology driven primarily by anger, envy, hate, and revenge.

If Hunter's analysis is right, I wonder, regardless of our approach, what might happen if instead of letting these negative things drive us to political action, we let something positive draw us. Again, Paul's words come to mind: "Set your minds on things above where Christ is, seated at the right hand of God" (Col. 3:1). How might focusing less on our enemies and more on our enthroned King shape the approach and tone of our politics?

For example, think of the way it shaped the apostle John in the book of Revelation. Most scholars agree that this book, filled with powerful, evocative images and symbols, was written to Christians during a time of intense persecution, opposition, and evil, when their world was falling apart. Yet according to Richard Bauckham, the throne of God is "the central symbol of the whole book."[18] In spite of the heavenly and earthly conflict swirling around him, he kept inviting his readers (and hearers) to behold God's throne in heaven and join in the worship surrounding it (Rev. 4:5, 7). In the book's final climactic scene (Rev. 22:3–5), we are once again brought back to the throne, where God's servants worship him and reign with him forever and ever.

In the midst of the conflict and upheaval around us, how might a greater certainty, conviction, and awareness of that unseen reality (the throne where Christ the King is reigning and being worshipped) shape our approach and affect the tone of our politics? And since that is where history is moving and the story ends (heaven and earth becoming one, all creation worshipping the King around the throne and reigning with him), how might working to prepare the world for its intended future positively define our political task?

4. Global

In the last fifty years we have witnessed an explosion of growth in the number of Christians worldwide, especially in Africa, Asia, and Latin America. However, most people on planet Earth still don't know that Jesus is King, and those in political power ignore his rule. In fact, according to the psalmist, "the nations conspire . . . The kings of the earth set themselves, and the rulers take counsel together, against the LORD and his anointed [king]" (Ps. 2:1–2). They stubbornly refuse to bow their knee to the king.

How then does Christ reign in such a world? In the final chapter of this book, when we consider the close relationship between Christ's ascension and the church's mission, we'll be directly seeking to answer that question. Here, however, we simply want to touch upon one particular aspect of mission closely tied to Christ's kingship.

"Sit at my right hand" says the Lord God, in Psalm 110:1, the verse that New Testament writers quoted so often in order to establish that Christ the Son had been installed as King. Then, in the next verse of the psalm there is a promise: "The LORD will extend your mighty scepter from Zion" (Ps. 110:2 NIV). The King can be confident, then, that his scepter, the sign of his rule and authority, will stretch out and increase.

But what exactly is that scepter? Christian commentators and theologians, as far back as Clement of Rome in the late first century, have said it is the preaching of the gospel. Contemporary theologians like T. F. Torrance agree. Following Clement, he maintained that through the proclamation of the gospel the ascended Christ "rules over the nations and all history . . . until he comes again to judge and renew his creation."[19]

Christ has commissioned us to be his witnesses (Acts 1:8). We have been sent forth as his ambassadors to proclaim the good news that Jesus is King and call upon others to submit to his rule. According to Tim Chester and Jonny Woodrow, our job, as heralds of the King, is to "go to the citizens of a country and say that a king is coming who rightly claims their allegiance. Those who currently rule them are usurpers and tyrants. But the true king is coming and He will be king. He will reign."[20]

Of course, this message has always been scandalous and offensive, and especially so in an age of hyperindividualism, relativism, and pluralism like ours. How can you dare be so exclusive and dogmatic, so harsh and unfair? Aren't there various kings we can choose from, depending on which one best suits us? And just look around—how, in this kind of world, can you claim he is reigning at all?

Richard Neuhaus described the difficulty and challenge of our mission well: "We are premature ambassadors, having arrived at the court before the sovereignty of our king has been recognized. It is awkward, of course, and our authority is very much in question. We must resist the temptation to relieve the awkwardness by accepting a lesser authority from another kingdom."[21]

Given our predicament, and coupled with growing opposition and pressure, how easy it is to keep silent or to dilute the gospel message to make it more palatable to our hearers. And how crucial it is, if we are to faithfully proclaim it, to keep our eyes fixed on our King and our minds set on things above, where Christ is, seated at God's right hand.

Questions for Personal and Group Reflection

1. The ascension means this: Jesus is now reigning as King. How does your awareness of that help you live in the face of the many things in our world that seem to contradict and deny his kingship?

2. What are the "floods" in your life where you are prone to fear and worry and yet where you need to declare that the Lord Jesus "sits enthroned as king forever" (Ps. 29:10)?

3. Have there been times in your life when you surrendered an area of your life to Jesus and began to allow him to reign in that area as King? What did you discover when you did that? In what present unsurrendered area of your life is Jesus asking you to allow him to reign as King? Are you afraid to let him be your King in that area? Why? What will it take for you to let him reign in that part of your life?

4. Pray for Christ's church around the world, particularly in those places where it is being attacked, threatened, and persecuted. Remind Christ of his promise to build, protect, and preserve his church (Matt. 16:18). Pray boldly on the basis of that promise.

5. How should Christians seek to extend Christ's rule in the public and political realms? What mistakes do they often make in attempting to do that? How might our politics be Christ-centered and positively, not negatively, driven?

6. Pray for Christians around the world as they seek to extend Christ's scepter by proclaiming the gospel and announcing that Christ is King. Pray especially for those who preach each week. How and where are you being called to be a witness and proclaim the good news?

CHAPTER THREE

Exalted Humanity

> But filled with the Holy Spirit, [Stephen] gazed into
> heaven and saw the glory of God and Jesus standing
> at the right hand of God. "Look," he said, "I see the
> heavens opened and the Son of Man standing at the
> right hand of God!"
>
> —ACTS 7:55–56

Just before he was stoned to death and became the first Christian martyr, Stephen had a vision of the ascended Christ. "I see the Son of Man standing at God's right hand," he exclaimed.

Commonly used as a title for Jesus in the Gospels, this is the only other place in the New Testament where he is called the Son of Man. Traditionally, going back to the church fathers, it has been understood as a title that emphasizes his full humanity. Jesus is therefore both Son of God (fully divine) and Son of Man (fully human). And although biblical scholars today have convincingly shown it had a different and wider range of meaning in first-century Judaism,[1] I agree with those who still maintain that "the old understanding of the phrase, as a reference to the real humanity of our Lord, contains an essential element of truth."[2]

So that's how I'm going to use Stephen's description—the Son of Man at God's right hand—in this chapter. It captures the staggering truth we want to focus on: *Because Jesus is ascended, humanity has been exalted and brought into the life of God*. Theologian Peter Toon summed it up well: "For now there is in heaven, in the very life of God himself, a glorified humanity belonging to the eternal Son and a humanity of the same essence as shared by the whole human race. Now created human beings can be drawn nearer to God than can the holy angels, for the former possess the same human nature as the Son possesses, and so in and through him they can draw near to God."[3]

When Jesus ascended into heaven, he brought our humanity with him. As A. W. Tozer explained in a sermon, Jesus took our human nature "into the Godhead." There human nature was "received, embraced, welcomed, and enthroned at the right hand of the Father."[4]

In the miracle of the incarnation he became flesh of our flesh and bone of our bone (John 1:14). We sing during Advent and Christmas, "Veiled in flesh the Godhead see; hail th'incarnate Deity."[5] But what about after his death and resurrection? Was his human flesh like a loose outer garment he had put on but now took off? In returning to heaven, did he no longer need or want it? What Stephen saw gives us the answer. The fact that the Son of Man is at God's right hand means that the perfect union with humanity, which had begun in the incarnation, *continues in heaven and throughout eternity.* As Charles Wesley expressed it in another of his ascension hymns, "Though returning to his throne . . . Still He calls mankind His own."[6]

In his book *Jesus Ascended,* Gerrit Dawson went to great lengths to make this point. He quoted theologians like Karl Barth who stated that Christ the Son maintains our humanity, "to all eternity. . . It is clothing which He does not put off. It is His temple which He does not leave. It is the form which He does not lose."[7]

Dawson underscored this because of the Gnostic tendencies in much of Christian thinking that have tended to spiritualize the ascension.[8] How can earthly, corruptible, and decaying human flesh, it is argued, be taken up to heaven? There is no place for it there. Although the eternal Son of God assumed flesh when he became incarnate, in returning to heaven he must have sloughed it off and left it behind. Only spiritual, non-material things are fit for heaven.

However, as Dawson carefully demonstrated, ancient church fathers like Tertullian, Augustine, and John Chrysostom consistently rejected such thinking. Tertullian, for example, stood against those whom he said "excluded from . . . the court of heaven itself, all flesh and blood whatsoever." He declared, to the contrary, that, "Jesus is still sitting there at the right hand of the Father, man, yet God . . . flesh and blood, yet purer than ours."[9]

To be sure, Christ is in heaven as a *spiritual* man with a glorified, *spiritual* body. Hence it is a body and, unlike our present human bodies, is no longer subject to corruption and decay. Yet it is a body nonetheless. And as theologian T. F. Torrance insisted, it is a body that makes him not less human but "more fully and truly human than any other humanity we know, for it was humanity in which all that attacks and undermines creaturely being is vanquished."[10] The fact, then, that Christ has a spiritual body doesn't mean he is less body, but more truly and completely body, for his physical existence has been redeemed from all that would destroy it.

In his heavenly existence, he therefore remains truly human. He does not slough off his humanity, but fully retains it. Neither is his humanity swallowed up in an infinite ocean of divinity. "When he was lifted up into heaven," as Barth maintained, "He was not deified, or assumed into the Godhead . . . but placed as man at the side of God, in direct fellowship with Him, in full participation in His glory."[11]

The ascension, then, is not an "excarnation,"[12] but as Peter Atkins suggested, is "the other end of incarnation doctrine."[13] It means that the incarnation continues, yes, even expands, in that we who are joined to Christ are now able to enter into the life of God. For, as the church fathers consistently emphasized, if the one who sits at God's right hand is not still fully human (as well as fully God), we will never be able to "enter the veil" and sit there with him. Dawson therefore summed it up like this: "The fully human one has gone within the veil in our name and even in our skin. United to him by the Spirit, to the one who remains united to us, we may follow where he has gone."[14]

His exaltation, and the exaltation of his humanity, thus opens the way for our exaltation, and the exaltation of our humanity. There is a Son of Man at God's right hand! The dust of the earth has been lifted to the throne of heaven. The ascension of Jesus is therefore the fore-taste and guarantee of our ascension to our originally designated royal status (Psalm 8). As Paul insisted, "Just as we have borne the image of the man of dust [Adam], we will also bear the image of the man of heaven [Christ]" (1 Cor. 15:49). Christopher Wordsworth (1807–1885) captured it beautifully in a verse of one of his hymns:

> Thou hast raised our human nature
> On the clouds to God's right hand;
> There we sit in heavenly places,
> There with thee in glory stand.
> Jesus reigns, adored by angels,
> Man with God is on the throne,
> Mighty Lord, in thine ascension,
> We by faith behold our own.[15]

Think of it! In the incarnation, God honors and affirms humanity by coming down and becoming human in the person of his Son. Yet in the ascension, God goes even further by raising our human nature and taking it into himself. Humanity is taken up into divinity so that now and forever, as Wordsworth said, "Man with God is on the throne."

Humanity Crowned with Glory and Honor

The ascension, then, reveals what high regard God has for humanity. There is a Son of Man at God's right hand! Unfortunately, however, God's high regard stands in marked contrast to the negative views of the material world, the body, and the human propagated in many Christian circles. As we turn to consider the practical implications of this important element of ascension doctrine, let us begin by acknowledging that far too often among orthodox and evangelical Christians, the material is set over against the spiritual, the body is portrayed as the enemy of the spirit, and the human is viewed as an obstacle to the divine. As John Stott observed, there is a "lingering evangelical asceticism" rooted in a "world-denying Gnosticism" that "has not yet been altogether eradicated from our theology and practice."[16]

To be sure, humanity is fallen and the image of God deeply marred as a result of sin. Scripture states that the unredeemed flesh is hostile to God (Gal. 5:17) and must be put to death in us (Rom. 8:13). Nevertheless, by sending his own Son in the likeness of sinful flesh (Rom. 8:3), by dwelling among us in human form, and taking our humanity to heaven, God has, in Charles Williams's wonderful phrase, "forever hallowed the flesh."[17] The final verdict on fallen human nature has been declared: God intends to redeem and restore it to its original created purpose.

Through the incarnation and ascension, God, who is Spirit, has become forever identified with embodied humanity. Spirit does not despise matter. That's why Christianity, as Archbishop William Temple was fond of saying, is the most materialistic religion in the world. For not only did God create the material world and call it good, but when it had become corrupted through humanity's sin, God assumed matter by sending his own Son in a human body and ascending with a glorified human body. God then intends to redeem our bodies, the material side of our existence, as well as our souls and spirits. Every time we affirm, with the Apostles' Creed, "I believe in the resurrection of the body" we are, in effect, declaring that.

True Christian spirituality, therefore, celebrates the material dimensions of creaturely existence. It is an *earthy* spirituality. Dietrich Bonhoeffer was concerned that well-intentioned Christians often drove an erroneous, unbiblical wedge between the sacred and the secular, the spiritual and the material, the heavenly and the earthly. "I fear that Christians who stand with only one leg on earth," he wrote while in prison, "also stand with only one leg in heaven."[18] Together, the incarnation and the ascension summon us to fix both legs on earth so that we can fix both legs in heaven where the Son of Man is at God's right hand.

Recognizing God's affirmation of the human in the incarnation and ascension also forms the basis of an authentic and robust Christian humanism. If God so values humanity that he joins himself to it by assuming and then exalting human flesh, how can we consider valuing it less? Thomas Merton spelled out this connection well:

> If the Word of God assumed a human nature and became a man, in all things like other men except sin, if he gave his life to unite the human race to God in his mystical body, then surely there must be an authentic humanism which is not only acceptable to Christians but is essential to the Christian mystery itself . . . In defending the natural law, the civic rights of men, the rights of human reason, the cultural values of diverse civilizations, scientific study and techniques, medicine, political science, and a thousand other good things in the natural order, the church is expressing her profoundly Christian humanism, or, in other words, her concern for man in all his wholeness and integrity as a creature and as the image of God . . . The salvation of man does not mean that he must divest himself of all that is human: that he must discard his reason, his love of beauty, his desire for friendship, his need

for human affection, his reliance on protection, order, and justice in society, his need to work and eat and sleep.

A Christianity that despises these fundamental needs of man is not truly worthy of the name.[19]

The fact God has assumed and exalted humanity in the incarnation and ascension calls us, then, to work for the protection, advancement, and celebration of all that is truly human in the world, and to stand and fight against all that is inhuman.

Embracing Our Humanity

Repeating what A. W. Tozer said, because Jesus is ascended as the Son of Man in heaven, humanity has been "received, embraced, welcomed, and enthroned at the right hand of God."[20] And if God so loves and values the human, dare we call "unclean" what God has called "clean" (Acts 10:15 NLT)? If God esteems our humanity so highly, how can we insist on despising it?

Yet how often in our personal lives is that exactly what we do! For the past few decades, as I've engaged in spiritual counsel with seminary students, especially in the ministry of healing prayer, I have come to realize how deeply rooted self-rejection is in so many of us. When I first read his *Life of the Beloved*, I was surprised when Henri Nouwen insisted that self-rejection is "the greatest enemy of the spiritual life" because it contradicts the truth that we are beloved of God.[21] Over the years, however, I have come to believe he is right. So often, as I have sought to help people experience more deeply their belovedness in Christ, we have bumped up against hindrances rooted in their unwillingness to accept and embrace themselves and their humanity.

Similar to Nouwen, Leanne Payne considered our inability to accept ourselves one of the three main barriers (along with an inability to receive God's forgiveness and an inability to forgive others) to spiritual and emotional wholeness in Christ. She insisted that proper self-acceptance is a Christian virtue and quotes Romano Guardini, the Catholic philosopher-theologian: "The act of self-acceptance is the root of all things. I must agree to be the person who I am. Agree to have the qualifications which I have. Agree to live within the limitations set for me. The clarity and the courageousness of this acceptance is the foundation of all existence."[22]

We said earlier that there is a fallen, sinful self, which Scripture commands us to deny (Mark 8:34) and put to death (Rom. 6:6; Eph. 4:22–3). But there is also a new self—our authentic human self—which is beloved of God and to be accepted and nourished (Eph. 4:24). However, as Payne suggested, "If we are busy hating that soul that God loves and is in the process of straightening out, we cannot help others—our minds will be riveted on ourselves—not on Christ who is our wholeness."[23]

The true self, whom God loves and we too must accept and love, is a finite, embodied human self with limitations, boundaries, qualifications, weaknesses, and inadequacies. That self, however, is often the very self we despise and reject.

Tim, a seasoned pastor, expressed it to me like this:

> I have always seen myself as "slightly less than," like the sixth man on the basketball team or the second fiddle in the orchestra. So I didn't like myself and believed there was something wrong with me. But is there anything inherently wrong with being sixth man or playing second fiddle? Aren't they good and necessary parts that contribute to the well-being of the team or the orchestra?
>
> Because I could never believe that about the particular part I was destined to play, I have struggled to embrace the completely unique and gifted person God has created me to be. I've rejected and hated myself because of my human limitations and because I wasn't someone else.

Which of your human limitations—physical, intellectual, emotional, familial, social, racial, cultural—have you been ashamed of or despised? Jesus, said the writer of Hebrews, is *"not ashamed* to call [us] brothers and sisters" (Heb. 2:11, italics mine). Since we are "flesh and blood, he himself likewise shared the same things" (Heb. 2:14). In his incarnation, he became fully human, and when he ascended, he unashamedly refused to rid himself of his humanity. Instead, he took humanity to heaven and enthroned it at God's right hand. He is not ashamed of his humanity. Should we then be ashamed of ours?

I'll never forget praying with a student we'll call Leslie. She was ashamed of and despised her gender. When she was a child, it had often been the cause of ridicule and hurt. She said:

> My father was stern. He would scold me and humiliate me for crying so much. "Girls are too sensitive," he would chide. "Quit crying and get control of yourself."
>
> There were also several boys at school who bullied me constantly. Compared to them I was so small. There was no way I could defend myself. And then when I would burst into tears, they would tease and torment me all the more. It was all because I was a girl and so small, so weak and overly emotional. If I had been a boy, I could have handled it and wouldn't have been so hurt. I grew up despising those things about myself and was determined to suppress my emotional side. I vowed that I would never appear weak and I would never let myself feel or express my emotions. I hated those things about myself and was mad at God for making me that way.

Leslie was very intelligent and a straight A student. She became an expert at "living out of her head" and suppressing her emotions. That was how she maintained control and kept herself from getting hurt. But her self-protective strategy also prevented her from forming close relationships and experiencing deep emotions.

One day my prayer partner and I witnessed a wonderful time of transformation and healing in Leslie. As she prayed, she renounced the vows she had made and repented for calling "unclean" those things about herself which God had called "clean." Then, as we led her, she positively chose to embrace the person she had been created to be: a woman with great gifts and strengths, but also a woman with limitations and weaknesses that made her susceptible to pain and suffering. In response to her prayer, I found myself praying authoritatively over her the words Jesus had spoken to Jairus's daughter, "Little girl, arise!" (Mark 5:41).

As we watched, something shifted in Leslie. She began to connect with parts of herself from which she had cut herself off. Hard and cold places in her heart softened and melted before our eyes. Broken chords began to vibrate. There was richer color in her face, and a deeper joy in her eyes. The Lord was surely in our midst and we could only praise and thank him for what he was doing for his beloved daughter.

The Son of Man is at God's right hand! Belief in the ascension, rightly understood, is a foundation for accepting and embracing our humanity with all its qualifications, imperfections, and limitations. God thinks so highly of humanity that he not only joins himself to it but raises and exalts it. How can we despise the unique person we are whom God so prizes? The doctrine of the ascension thus leads to a proper self-love and self-acceptance.

An Invitation to Humility

Some, as we've noted, consider such self-acceptance to be a Christian virtue. I wonder, however, if what they are really describing is humility, what John Cassian called the "queen of all the virtues."[24] For contrary to the common misconception, humility is *not* self-depreciation, but *true self-appreciation*. It doesn't mean thinking less of yourself than you ought to think. Rather, humility is viewing yourself according to what God says about you and your humanity in the light of the ascension. Tim and Leslie, the persons we described earlier, were not being humble because they thought less of themselves than they should have. For self-acceptance, understood as true self-appreciation, is an essential part of humility.

Of course, being humble also means, in the words of Paul, that you not "think of yourself more highly than you ought to think, but to think with sober judgment" (Rom. 12:3). Ever since we believed the serpent's lie that we can be like God, we humans have exalted ourselves and pushed God off the throne. Taking charge, we construct grandiose false selves where everything revolves around us. In essence, that's what pride is and why it's chief among the seven deadly sins.

The ascension, however, confronts human pride and calls us to humility. It is the Son of *Man* who is at

God's right hand. So even though our humanity has been exalted to share in God's life and glory, we always remain human. The boundary line between divinity and humanity will never be blurred or erased. Christ's glorified humanity does not dissolve in an ocean of divinity, nor will we ever merge with divinity.

Christ's ascension exalts humanity, but it also keeps humanity in its rightful place. So it confronts pride and calls us to humility as true self-appreciation. Contrary to the serpent's false narrative, we are not divine, nor will we ever become divine. We are and always will be human. So we shouldn't think more highly of ourselves than we ought to think.

Consider also how the *manner* of the ascension demonstrates humility. "When it says, 'He ascended,'" Paul explained, "What does it mean but that he also descended into the lower parts of the earth? He who descended is the same one who ascended far above all the heavens, so that he might fill all things" (Eph. 4:9–10). To say then that Christ *ascended* into heaven also means, according to Paul, that he *descended* into the depths. The two are bound together. You can't have one without the other, ascent without descent, glorification without humiliation.

Like Paul, the apostle John was careful to make the same point. In John's gospel, Jesus said to Nicodemus, "No one has ascended into heaven except the one who descended from heaven, the Son of Man" (John 3:13). Moreover, according to John, Christ's ascension begins, paradoxically, with his being lifted up by his death (John 3:13–14; 8:28; 12:32–34). His exaltation from humiliation to glory happens *through the cross*.[25]

It is interesting how Bernard of Clairvaux, the great "spiritual doctor" of the medieval church, also emphasized this. In one of his Ascension Sermons, he quoted Paul's words: "Christ who descended is also the very one who ascended" (Eph. 4:10). Then he added, "And I myself believe he ascended in this very act of descending, for it was necessary that Christ descend in order that we might be taught to ascend."[26]

Contrary to Christ, Satan declared, "I will ascend to heaven; I will raise my throne above the stars of God" (Isa. 14:13). Likewise, all of us have sought to ascend, to be like God by exalting ourselves in numerous ways. What happens as a result? Bernard said, we "[fall] instead of ascending, because humility alone exalts and alone leads to life."[27]

How then do we ascend? As the psalmist inquired, "Who shall ascend the hill of the LORD? And who shall stand in his holy place?" (Ps. 24:3). According to Bernard, Christ establishes the pattern for us. Because he descended so low, even to the point of dying on a cross, he was therefore exalted so highly (Phil. 2:8–9).

So Bernard exhorted us to, "'Go and do the same.' You cannot ascend unless you descend, because it is fixed as by an everlasting law, that 'everyone who exalts himself shall be humbled, and one who humbles himself shall be exalted.'"[28] To ascend in God, we must descend from our hills of pride, self-centeredness, and independence. In preparing the way of the Lord, "every mountain and hill [must] be made low" (Isa. 40:4). It is the path of downward mobility that leads upward.

During the last years of her brief life, Thérèse of Lisieux (1873–1897) profoundly lived out this downward pattern in the convent where she served as a nun. This "Little Flower" was soon canonized as a saint (1925) and later declared by Pope John Paul II as a doctor of the Roman Catholic Church (1997). She described it as her "Little Way" to sanctity and love. As she wrote, "The only way to make progress in the way of love is to remain always very little; this is what I have done, so now I can sing with Saint John of the Cross:

> *And as I sank so low, so low,*
> *So high so high, did upward go,*
> *That in the end I reached my prey.*[29]

As we sink "low, so low" and "remain always very little," then "high so high, [we] upward go." I wonder what that might specifically mean in your life and mine. Where are we being called to ascend by descending?

Questions for Personal and Group Reflection

1. According to the discussion at the beginning of the chapter, in relation to our humanity, how does the ascension further and complete what was begun in

the incarnation (the Word became flesh and dwelt among us)?

2. Do you agree that negative views of the material world, the body, and the human have often been propagated by Christians? Why or why not?

3. In what specific ways has God called you to work for the protection and advancement of all that is truly human in the world? Where has he called you to stand and fight against all that is inhuman?

4. Which of your human limitations—physical, intellectual, emotional, familial, social, racial, cultural—have you been ashamed of or despised? Have you called "unclean" what the Lord has said is "clean"? Which of your limitations are you being called upon to accept?

5. Where in your life is Christ calling you to ascend by descending? Where is he calling you to be "little" and setting before you the path of humility?

CHAPTER FOUR

Always with Us

When he had said this, as they were watching, he was lifted up, and a cloud took him out of their sight. While he was going and they were gazing up toward heaven, suddenly two men in white robes stood by them.

—Acts 1:9-10

"He who descended is the same one who ascended far above all the heavens, so that he might fill all things" (Eph. 4:10). We were discussing the first part of this verse at the end of the last chapter in thinking about humility. To ascend like Christ, we have to descend. As the Scripture says, those who humble themselves will be exalted. However, we intentionally waited until now to discuss the last part of the verse where Paul told us why Jesus ascended: *so that he might fill all things.*

That is the focus of this chapter. The ascension means that Christ, who entered into heaven, can now be personally present, not just in one place at a time, as during his earthly life, but in all places at all times. Through the Holy Spirit, the ascended Jesus who is in heaven is here, now, in person, with us every moment, every day, everywhere. That means he is always with us!

"So that he might fill all things." One day, as F. B. Meyer (1847–1929), the great evangelist and Bible teacher, was reflecting on that phrase, suddenly it dawned on him what it meant: "When I saw that, only the other day, I said to myself: 'Jesus Christ is literally in this room. It is true that He is at the right hand of God, but this is only to allow Him the more easily to fill my heart, my need, my life. He is the very same as when Martha and Mary welcomed Him to their home in Bethany . . . He is the same loving, tender Savior as when the children flocked around His knees, and His tears brimmed over at the grave of His friend.'"[1]

The ascension means Christ's ever-present personal presence. Through the Holy Spirit, he is here now with us. Theologian T. F. Torrance explained it like this: "The ascension of Christ is thus an ascension to fill all things with himself, so that in a real sense he comes again in the ascension. He had to go away in one mode of his presence that he might come again in this mode of presence, leaving us in the mode of man's presence to man, and returning to us in the mode of God's presence to man, and thus not leaving man bereft of himself."[2]

Ascension and Presence[3]

There are a number of ways the New Testament writers connect Christ's ascension and his presence with us. For example, in describing his ascension, Luke said "a *cloud* took him out of their sight" as the disciples "were gazing up toward *heaven*" (Acts 1:9–10, italics mine). The cloud, most scholars agree, is reminiscent of the cloud which descended upon the tabernacle constructed by Moses and the people in the wilderness (Exod. 40:34) and the temple built by Solomon (1 Kings 8:10–11). With the cloud came the glory—the Shekinah—the manifest presence of God. "Thus, to enter it," noted Peter Toon, "was to go into the holy of holies, the immediate presence of the Lord."[4]

Heaven, the dwelling place of God in creation, is also closely associated in Scripture with the fullness of the divine presence. In reference to Christ's ascension, notice how the writer of Hebrews linked the two together: "He entered heaven itself, now to appear for us in God's presence" (Heb. 9:24 NIV). Heaven is a place that is totally pervaded by God's glory. In fact, according to K. C. Thompson, "What makes heaven Heaven is the immediate and perceptible presence of God."[5]

"He ascended *into heaven*" the Creed says. That means Christ has been brought back to the place of the fullness of God's presence. When he became incarnate, the eternal Son voluntarily laid that aside (Phil. 2:5–11) and limited himself to an awareness and experience of God's presence through human faculties and a human consciousness. The ascension means that the period of self-renunciation and self-limitation has come to an end. It means, according to J. G. Davies, that the eternal Son's "consciousness of absolute unity and communion with the Father, which in varying manners and degrees, most notably shown in the cry of dereliction on the Cross, had been limited by the flesh, was fully restored."[6]

Moreover, because Christ is *in heaven*, he is no longer subject to the limits of space and time as when he was on earth. Now, because heaven touches earth tangentially, our risen Lord can be everywhere at once! It means, according to N. T. Wright, that, "Jesus is available, accessible, without people having to travel to a particular spot on earth to find him."[7] We don't need a time machine to transport us into the past or future to reach him. Now, as theologian Anthony Kelly stated, "The ascended Christ occupies a region of divine accessibility in which all times are now contemporaneous with him, and all places open to his presence."[8]

In his ascension hymn, Brian Wren conveyed this truth well:

> Christ is alive!
> No longer bound to distant years in Palestine,
> he comes to claim the here and now
> and dwell in every place and time.[9]

The ascended Christ is therefore present (here) in the present (now).

During the Great Thanksgiving, in the oft-used liturgy for the Lord's Supper, the congregation proclaims the mystery of faith: "Christ has died, Christ is risen, Christ will come again." That mystery stands revealed before us "where Christ is, seated at the right hand of God." There, all three time dimensions—past, present, and future—are gathered into one and made present to us. Yesterday and someday converge with today. Christ is "there," seated at the right hand of God, and because we have been "raised with Christ" (Col. 3:1) and our lives are "hidden with Christ" (Col. 3:3), through the Holy Spirit, we are "there" too. Go figure!

My longtime spiritual mentor and friend, Dennis Kinlaw, told how he became aware of this when, as a young pastor, he decided to preach a sermon on the ascension. In preparing, he found himself pondering two questions: When Jesus ascended, *how far* did he go? And *how long* did it take him to get there. As he reflected on them, he broke out in laughter. For he realized, "How far?" and "How long?" are space and time questions. Furthermore, since he created space and time, Christ transcends them. He isn't bound by space and time. In fact, he is not *in* them; they are *in* him.

As Paul said in his sermon on Mars Hill in Athens, "He is not far from any one of us. For in him we live and move and exist" (Acts 17:27–28 NLT). "Suddenly," said

Kinlaw, "I found that I had a sense of his nearness that I had never had before."[10]

Here Now with Us

He ascended *into heaven*—that's what it meant for Jesus. He has returned to the "place" from which he is able to be present in all times and places. What then does it mean for those who are in Christ and have been raised up and seated with him in the heavenly realms (Eph. 2:6)? It means that while we are "here" on earth, through the Holy Spirit we are also "there" in heaven with him. Consequently, as T. F. Torrance wrote, "Christ is nearer to us than we are to ourselves, and we who live and dwell on earth are yet made to sit with Christ 'in heavenly places,' partaking of the divine nature in him."[11]

Christ's prayer, "Father, I want these whom you have given me to be with me where I am" (John 17:24 NLT), is fulfilled in part even now. "Through his grace," as Kinlaw came to realize, "God has made it possible for me to live in His presence every moment, so that heaven actually begins for me right now in time and space."[12] Think of it, even now while we're "here" we're also "there" with him!

What's more, because Christ is in heaven, he's present here, not as an ethereal, impersonal abstraction, like the force in *Star Wars*. He is *personally* present—at all times and in all places—on earth with us. When Jesus commissioned his disciples just before he ascended, he told them: "And remember, *I am with you always*, to the end of the age" (Matt. 28:20, italics mine). Recognizing and living according to his promised, personal presence is a tremendous spiritual blessing and asset. Jesus is always with us in actual presence as a person in relation with us. As we sing in the words of the familiar hymn, "Great Is Thy Faithfulness": "Thine own dear presence to cheer and to guide."[13] The fact that we are with him in heaven and he is with us on earth means we can live every moment of our lives in the holy of holies presence of God.

When God told Moses it was time to break camp at Mt. Sinai and go up to Canaan, Moses complained, "See, you have said to me, 'Bring up this people'; but you have not let me know whom you will send with me" (Exod. 33:12). Then God responded to Moses with this wonderful promise: "My presence will go with you, and I will give you rest" (Exod. 33:14).

Now, however, because Jesus is ascended, that promise is more profoundly true and significant for us than it was for Moses himself. For he lived under the old covenant, where only once a year the high priest was allowed to enter the Holy of Holies, the very presence of God. But we live under the new covenant, where Jesus, our Great High Priest, has opened up a "new and living way" (Heb. 10:20). Now we have access to the Holy of Holies; we can live in the very presence of God every moment of every day.

In "Alleluia, Sing to Jesus," Gregory Dix's wonderful ascension hymn, there is a verse that captures it well:

Alleluia! not as orphans are we left in sorrow
   now;
Alleluia! He is near us, faith believes, nor questions how;
Though the cloud from sight received him when
   the forty days were o'er,
Shall our hearts forget his promise, 'I am with
   you evermore'?[14]

To be sure, we may not be consciously aware of God
or have a tangible sense of Christ's presence. We may be
feeling just the opposite: as if Christ were far away and
very absent. But that doesn't change the fact that we
are seated in the heavenly realms with Christ and he is
always with us. In reality—whether it is the unseen or the
seen real—Jesus is as near to us now as he was to John,
when the Beloved Apostle laid his head on his breast
during the Last Supper. He's as present now as he was to
Mary, when she sat at his feet, listening to him teach in
her home in Bethany.

We never have to wonder where Christ is. We don't
have to beg him to come on the scene. He is present with
us even when he seems most absent. No matter how
unholy the situation we may seem to be in, we can be
confident he's with us. We are in the Holy of Holies with
him! A. W. Tozer summed it up well: "Ransomed men
and women need no longer pause in fear to enter the
Holy of Holies. God wills that we should push on into
His presence and live our whole life there. This is to be
known to us in conscious experience. It is more than a

doctrine to be held; it is a life to be enjoyed every moment of every day."[15]

If only we could seize hold of this truth and reality! We are with Christ and Christ is with us. It would transform our lives and our ministry for Christ.

Always Before Us

The psalmist declared, "I keep the LORD always before me; because he is at my right hand, I shall not be moved. Therefore my heart is glad and my soul rejoices; my body also rests secure. . . . In your presence there is fullness of joy; in your right hand are pleasures forevermore" (Ps. 16:8–9, 11). All these things—stability, gladness, security, joy, pleasure—flow into our lives as a result of being in Christ's presence, right here, right now.

Sadly, however, we can be oblivious and unaware of it, living as if it weren't so, acting as if we are all alone. Jacob had a dream in which God showed him angels ascending and descending on a ladder connecting heaven and earth. When he awoke, he cried out, "Surely the LORD is in this place—and I did not know it!" (Gen. 28:16). That was his problem. Often it is ours too. Christ is personally present *all* the time, 24/7, but we are unaware of it.

So it's crucial for us to do what the psalmist was careful to do: "I keep the LORD always before me." We must be receptive and attentive, intentional and purposeful, about cultivating an awareness of Christ's presence. Of course, he is present whether we are aware of it or not, but our attentiveness to his presence isn't automatic. Although Christ is always present, paradoxically, his presence must be *sought*. So we are exhorted in another psalm to "seek the LORD and his strength; seek his presence continually" (Ps. 105:4). We must choose to be attentive and receptive to Christ's presence. Too often he is in the room speaking but we're not listening; he is leading but we're not following.

We must purpose, then, like the psalmist, to "keep the LORD always before" us and, as Paul instructed us, to "set our minds on things above" (Col. 3:2). We must strive, like Brother Lawrence, to "practice the presence of God" and like St. Patrick, to pray "Christ be with me, Christ within me, Christ behind me, Christ before me, Christ beside me, Christ beneath me, Christ above me."

As we turn now to consider some practical implications of his constant personal presence with us as a result of the ascension, let us think about some particular ways we can become attentive to his presence.

Seeking His Presence in the Likely Places

Thankfully, Jesus did not leave us in the dark about what we should do to seek his presence. There are certain places where he himself has promised to meet us. John Wesley (1703–1791), the founder of Methodism and the Wesleyan Christian tradition, called these appointed places "the means of grace."[16] They are the common, ordinary channels or means through which we become aware of his presence, the "likely places" where we encounter Christ.

According to Wesley, Christ himself ordained and instituted five such means of grace. First, *prayer*, in all its various forms, private and public, which he considered "the grand means of drawing near to God."[17] All the others are only useful when they are combined with or lead us to prayer. Second, *searching the Scriptures*, which included regularly reading the Bible, studying and meditating upon it, putting it into practice, and hearing it preached and taught. Third, *attendance at the Lord's Supper*, since, like the men on the Emmaus road, Christ's presence is known to us in the breaking of the bread (Luke 24:35). Fourth, *fasting*, since it was commanded by Christ (Matt. 6:16–18), intensifies our desire for God, and increases spiritual sensitivity. And fifth, what Wesley called *"Christian conferencing,"* i.e., conferencing or gathering with a few other Christians for fellowship, accountability, study, and prayer. He based this on Christ's promise that "where two or three are gathered in my name, I am there among them" (Matt. 18:20).

Wesley believed that these five means of grace, instituted by Christ himself, are the divinely appointed places of waiting. If then we are to be receptive and attentive to Christ's presence, we cannot neglect them. Indeed, we must *devote* ourselves to them.

Interestingly, they parallel the description of the activities of the earliest Christian community outlined in Acts 2:42: "They devoted themselves to the apostles' teaching [searching the Scriptures] and fellowship [Christian conference], to the breaking of bread [attendance at the Lord's Supper] and the prayers [prayer]." If we add to this the description of the congregation at Antioch (Acts 13:1–3), which was "worshiping the Lord and fasting," then we see that all five of Wesley's means were an integral, vital part of the life and practice of the earliest Christians.

Of course, you may be a part of a different Christian tradition and have never heard of John Wesley's means of grace. But regardless of how you describe them, I'm sure you have something similar in your tradition. All Christians everywhere recognize the crucial importance of spiritual disciplines, devotional practices, means of grace—call them what you will. There are also various other important practices we could discuss (Sabbath-keeping, the Divine Hours, *Lectio Divina*, and silence, to name a few).

In this there is broad consensus within the whole Christian tradition. These practices are absolutely indispensable for cultivating an awareness of and attentiveness to Christ's presence. We must regularly and habitually engage in them. If we are going to know the reality of his ascension presence, there simply is no other way.

When we neglect these means, disciplines, or practices, our faith—the conviction of things not seen (Heb. 11:1)—quickly dissipates and dissolves. Consequently, our awareness of Christ's love for us—so deep, passionate, and undeserved—soon fades. We forget his precious promises to us (2 Peter 1:4). Our conviction of "things above" (the unseen real) diminishes. Before we realize it, we are assuming and acting as if we are all alone—as if everything depends on us. Our faith spirals downward and anxiety, stress, frustration, and fear rises within us. As Oswald Chambers said, "Our problems come when we refuse to bank on the reality of his presence."[18]

So let me emphasize it again: we must seek his presence in these "likely places" where he has told us to meet him. *There is no other way.*

Christ's Presence in the Unlikely Places

But Christ's ascension to heaven means we can seek him in unlikely places too. Remember, he ascended, so that he can fill *all* things, *all* times, and *all* places. If we are attentive, every moment, every experience of life, no matter how ordinary or mundane it might seem, can open a door that ushers us into Christ's presence.

That's what Brother Lawrence, the seventeenth-century Carmelite friar, discovered as he made "the practice of the presence of God" in the midst of all his everyday activities the goal and ambition of his life. After several years, he came to the place where he could say, "The time of business does not with me differ from the time of prayer, and in the noise and clatter of my kitchen, while several persons are at the same time calling for different things, I possess God in as great tranquility as if I were upon my knees at the blessed sacrament."[19]

But practicing his presence is not only for extraordinary people like Brother Lawrence. Greg Boyd, in his helpful book *Present Perfect,* described how for the past several decades, with help from people like Brother Lawrence, Jean-Pierre de Caussade, and Frank Laubach, he has worked to do it in his own life.[20] We too can learn to practice the presence of Christ. Each moment, each experience of life, no matter how dull or ordinary, can become a Christophany if we learn to be attentive. In the midst of all our activities we must learn to pray, "Lord Jesus, I acknowledge you are present here. Make me aware of your presence."

Another significant but unlikely place where we can seek Christ's presence is in the face of human need. In the parable of the last judgment, both the sheep and the goats—those who were received and those who were rejected—were puzzled and surprised: "Lord, when was it that we saw you hungry or thirsty or a stranger or naked or sick or in prison?" (Matt. 25:44). He had been there all along, yet they had failed to see him. But where was he? They wanted to know. Then the answer came: "As you did not do it to one of the least of these, you did not do it to me" (Matt. 25:45).

Christ meets us in the faces of the poor, the broken, the hungry, the lonely, the disenfranchised. When we reach out to them, we encounter him there. So Mother Teresa and her sisters discovered in serving the poor in Calcutta. While she held a dying leper in her arms, she was face-to-face with Christ. As the sisters ministered to the broken and the dying, they were ministering to their present-yet-unseen Lord. That's what made their ministry to the dying unique, she said, as distinct from social work: "We do it to a Person."[21]

In the face of human need, our natural tendency is to turn and look the other way. Like the priest and the Levite in Jesus' parable of the good Samaritan, we would rather "pass by on the other side" (Luke 10:31–32). Jesus, however, said, "Don't turn away or keep your distance. Look deep into the eyes of your hurting brothers and sisters. Reach out and touch them. You'll be touching me if you do."

Christ is ascended *so that he can fill all things*—all times and places with his presence, the likely and the unlikely places.

Joining Him in Ministry

Earlier, in the light of Psalm 16, we mentioned some of the benefits that flow to us when we are receptive and attentive to his personal presence: stability, security, gladness, joy, and pleasure (Ps. 16:8–11). But finding Christ in the midst of human need leads us to consider another benefit at the heart of all authentic Christian service and ministry: we get to join the risen Jesus himself in what he is doing in the world today!

Too often, as we go about the business of serving him, we pray and ask Christ to help us and bless what we're doing for him. In the light of the reality of his ascension presence, however, our understanding shifts. Now instead of praying, "Lord, help me, bless my efforts," we pray, "Lord, you are here working. Use me. Do what you want to do through me to accomplish your purposes. And don't let me get in the way of what you're doing."

In the end, isn't that what counts? Not what we're doing, but what the risen, ascended Christ is doing through us. Yet how will we know what Christ desires to do or is doing in a particular situation unless we are intentional in being attentive to his presence? I've written about this at greater length in *Ministry in the Image of God* where I stressed that the ministry and service in which we are involved is *Christ's* not ours.[22] We get to join him as his ministry and service continues in the world today.

And speaking of benefits, since it's *his* ministry, the burden is Christ's, not ours. When we assume the burden of ministry, assuming it all depends on us, we take on a heavy burden we were never designed to carry. Remember, his yoke is easy and his burden is light (Matt. 11:30). Knowing that ministry and service is ultimately his burden brings rest to our souls (Matt. 11:29). And we discover another reason why in his presence there is fullness of joy!

Recently, someone who had read what I had written in *Ministry in the Image of God* decided to put it into practice. Here's how she described what happened:

> I work at a mental health hospital as a clinical counselor. In the past, my prayer, as I entered work, was always to ask Christ to lead me and guide me through my ministry, helping me to be a

vehicle, instead of a barrier. For one week I prayed instead that Christ would allow me to accompany him, asking him to fill me with the Holy Spirit and allow me to piggyback on his ministry.

It was the most exciting ministry with the most surprising results. The anxiety I usually experienced as I entered the building was gone. I was smiling and felt a power around me that felt unstoppable. My colleagues responded to me differently, often asking for guidance or consultations. And the clients prospered.

My days were filled with something bigger than I could have ever imagined. I liked coming to work. My journey became bigger than I am, because it *was* bigger than I am. I was tagging alongside Jesus through the Holy Spirit. This outward journey was making an incredible difference in my own life, and making an incredible difference in the lives of my clients.

The whole change led to a promotion for me to supervisor. My seven days has turned into an ongoing approach to ministry.

I certainly can't guarantee you a promotion if you try it! But I think I can guarantee that your load will be lighter. And your attentiveness to his presence, enriched and expanded as a result of Christ's ascension, will lead to anticipation and an awareness of something happening that is bigger than you are. For in his presence is fullness of joy.

Questions for Personal and Group Reflection

1. Have you ever had an experience like F. B. Meyer's, where you were deeply aware of the presence of Jesus with you? How did that experience affect you?

2. Which of John Wesley's five instituted means of grace (prayer, searching the Scriptures, attendance at the Lord's Supper, fasting, Christian conferencing—gathering in small groups for encouragement and accountabilty) have you found most helpful and meaningful in increasing your sense of Christ's presence? Which have you practiced least? What is Christ calling you to do in relation to the means of grace?

3. We can also experience the presence of Christ in "unlikely places"—like Brother Lawrence, in our ordinary, humdrum activities, and like Mother Teresa, in the face of human need. Have you had experiences where that has happened to you? In what unlikely places in your life is Christ inviting you to look for him and seek his presence?

4. How do you tend to approach Christian service and ministry? Is it primarily about asking Jesus to *help* you or asking Jesus to *use* you? What practical implication might the idea of you joining the present, risen, ascended Christ in his ministry have for your service and ministry?

CHAPTER FIVE

Power over Our Enemies

I was pushed hard, so that I was falling, but the LORD helped me. The LORD is my strength and my might; he has become my salvation. There are glad songs of victory in the tents of the righteous: "The right hand of the LORD does valiantly; the right hand of the LORD is exalted; the right hand of the LORD does valiantly."

—PSALM 118:13–16

A six-year-old boy and his father were out walking one evening as the sun was setting. The display of colors on the horizon was breathtakingly beautiful—unlike anything the young boy had ever seen before. "Wow!" he exclaimed. "Isn't that awesome! God must have painted that with his *left* hand."

His father was puzzled. "Why did you say his *left* hand," he asked.

"Well, at church on Sunday when we recite that creed," his son answered, "don't we say that Jesus is sitting *on* his *right* one!"

Not exactly! Jesus isn't sitting *on* the Father's right hand, but *at* the Father's right hand. His Father says to him, in the words of Psalm 110:1, "Sit at my right hand until I make your enemies a footstool for your feet" (NIV).

As the place of highest honor, the right hand of God is symbolic throughout Scripture with God's strength, power, and authority. For example, after God rescued the Israelites by parting the Red Sea, Moses declared, "Your right hand, O LORD, glorious in power—your right hand, O LORD, shattered the enemy" (Exod. 15:6). The psalmist extolled the greatness of God in similar fashion: "Powerful is your arm! Strong is your hand! Your right hand is lifted high in glorious strength" (Ps. 89:13 NLT). With his right hand, we are told, "the LORD does valiantly" (Ps. 118:15–16).

Christ's ascension to God's right hand means that he does valiantly too! As Paul declared, God demonstrated his power "when he raised [Christ] from the dead and seated him at his right hand in the heavenly places, far above all rule and authority and power and dominion . . . And he has put all things under his feet" (Eph. 1:20–22).

In spite of his triumph, however, many of Christ's enemies refuse to recognize his authority or submit to his rule. So from his position in heaven, seated at God's right hand, he works and watches and waits until that day when every knee will bow and every tongue confesses that he is Lord (Phil. 2:10–11). The writer of Hebrews, echoing Psalm 110:1, expressed it like this: "But when Christ had offered for all time a single sacrifice for sins, 'he sat down at the right hand of God,' and since then has been waiting 'until his enemies would be made a footstool for his feet'" (Heb. 10:12–13). A verse from Charles Wesley's hymn, "Rejoice, the Lord Is King!" also sums it up well:

> He sits at God's right hand,
> Till all His foes submit,
> And bow to His command,
> And fall beneath His feet.
> Lift up your heart, lift up your voice,
> Rejoice, again I say, rejoice.[1]

Here then is another significant consequence of the ascension: the power and authority to carry out the work of redemption and bring it to full and final consummation have been placed in Christ's radiant nail-scarred hands! As Jesus announced just before he ascended, "all authority in heaven and on earth has been given to me" (Matt. 28:18).

And, of course, this important facet of the ascension, which is the focus of this chapter, has profound implications for us. That's why Paul prayed that the Christians at Ephesus "will understand the incredible greatness of God's power *for us who believe him*" (Eph. 1:19 NLT, italics mine). The apostle wanted us to grasp that because all power and authority have been given to him, those who are in Christ share in it too. Having been raised up and seated with him in the heavenly realms (Eph. 2:6; Col. 3:1), the Father says to us what he says to the Son: "Sit at my right hand until I make your enemies a footstool for your feet" (Ps. 110:1 NIV).

Think about your life for a moment. Who or what are your *enemies*? They may include a broad range of things. Difficult circumstances you have to contend with; people who stand against you—some who have hurt you deeply; your own sins, failures, and inadequacies; physical and emotional infirmities you struggle with and endure; the world system which hates you because it hates Christ; Satan and all his demonic principalities.

We all have our share of enemies! At times they overwhelm us and seem to make us into a footstool for *their* feet. But Paul wanted us to remember that Christ is seated at God's right hand, and because we are seated with him, we can be "more than conquerors" (Rom. 8:37). In due time, our enemies will become a footstool for Christ's feet. Right-hand-of-God power and authority has been bestowed upon the ascended Christ, and those who are in him share in it too.

Ruling in Power in the Midst of Our Enemies

"Sit at my right hand, until I make your enemies a footstool for your feet" (Ps. 110:1 NIV). Throughout this book, we keep circling back to this verse—the most oft-quoted Old Testament verse in the New Testament.

But as we consider now what right-hand-of-God power might look like practically in our lives, I want us to pay particular attention to the verse that immediately follows: "The LORD will extend your mighty scepter from Zion, saying, 'Rule in the midst of your enemies!'" (Ps. 110:2 NIV).

I believe this wonderful promise—"You will rule in the midst of your enemies"—is not only for the ascended Christ. Since we are in Christ and therefore seated with him at God's right hand, it's a promise for us too!

Notice, however, it's not a promise that the Lord will get rid of our enemies. Someday, when Christ returns, that will happen, but not yet. Until then we will have enemies—enemies, as we've noted, that come in various shapes and sizes. So this is not a rose-garden promise to remove our enemies, but an invitation to *rule in the midst* of them. As David expressed it in the beloved Twenty-Third Psalm: "You prepare a table before me *in the presence of* my enemies" (v. 5, italics mine).

Though we have enemies, we can rule in the midst of them and be "more than conquerors" through Christ (Rom. 8:37). Having been raised up and seated with Christ "in the heavenly places" (Eph. 2:6; Col. 3:1), we are therefore at God's right hand, enthroned with Christ in the place of authority. That means we are no longer in a defensive, but an offensive position in relation to our enemies. We are in the midst of them but also looking *down* on them from above. Knowing that should cause us to rise up in confidence, boldness, and authority.

Remember the story of David and Goliath? Goliath was insulted that the Israelites would send out such a pathetic, unworthy opponent as David to fight him. He was infuriated when he saw that the man who had been sent out to fight him was "only a youth." "Am I a dog, that you come to me with sticks?" he taunted. "Come to me, and I will give your flesh to the birds of the air and to the wild animals of the field" (1 Sam. 17:43–44).

Goliath, the nine-foot giant, armed from head to toe, was an experienced, bloodthirsty warrior. David, the shepherd boy with only a sling, was obviously no match for him.

Yet when Goliath advanced toward him, what did David do? Tremble? Shake in his boots? Start backpedaling as fast as he could? No. Scripture says: "When the Philistine drew nearer to meet David, *David ran quickly toward the battle line to meet the Philistine*" (1 Sam. 17:48, italics mine).

Amazing! David didn't wait for the giant to initiate the combat. Instead he put his head down and charged toward Goliath. He didn't fight defensively, using his quickness and smaller size to avoid Goliath's attacks, hoping possibly to wear the giant down. No. David went on the offensive!

King Saul and David's older brothers were probably shaking their heads in dismay. How foolish could David be? The lowly shepherd boy must be delusional! Yet we know that wasn't the case. Why then was he so undaunted and courageous?

What David shouted to Goliath just before he charged toward him provides the answer: "You come to me with sword and spear and javelin; but I come to you in the name of the LORD of hosts" (1 Sam. 17:45). David's boldness and confidence was in the name of the one in whom he had come: *Yahweh Sabaoth*—the Lord of Hosts, *the Lord of Heaven's Armies*. That name, which occurs approximately two hundred ninety times in the Bible, is one of the most frequent divine names in Scripture.

David had set his mind on things above, on the one above, who sits on heaven's throne, who commands heaven's armies and reigns above the earth. Seen in that light, from the perspective of heaven, he doesn't look up at nine-foot Goliath; he looks down on him. Compared to David's God, the Lord of Hosts, Goliath was like a tiny flea on the rear end of an elephant!

After he defeated Goliath, David went on to become a mighty warrior, no doubt the greatest in all Israel's history. "Blessed be the LORD, my rock," he would declare, "who trains my hands for war, and my fingers for battle" (Ps. 144:1; cf. Ps. 18:34). Scripture describes his mighty exploits in significant detail.

But the reason David became a great warrior and subdued his enemies was because, first and foremost, he was a great worshipper. That was how he set his mind on things above. Before he learned to wield a sling or a sword, he first learned to play a harp. That's what we remember him for most: his worship songs found in the Psalms. So many of the individual psalms are attributed to him that Charles Spurgeon aptly titled his great devotional commentary on the Psalms *The Treasury of David*.[2]

The close connection between worship and warfare is hard to miss in many of them. Consider Psalm 27, for example. "Though an army encamp against me," David declared, "my heart shall not fear; though war rise up against me, yet I will be confident" (Ps. 27:3). He sure sounds like a confident warrior here!

But notice the following verse: "One thing I asked of the LORD, that will I seek after; to live in the house of the LORD all the days of my life, to behold the beauty of the LORD, and to inquire in his temple" (Ps. 27:4). Often that verse is quoted to underscore the centrality and the priority of worship. It's the "one thing" David desired.

And as a result of doing that "one thing," he exulted, "Now my head is lifted up above my enemies all around me, and I will offer in his tent sacrifices with shouts of joy; I will sing and make melody to the LORD" (Ps. 27:6).

David was a great warrior because he is a great worshipper! He was able to subdue his enemies because his head was lifted up above them. Because his eyes were focused on the Lord, while he was in the midst of his enemies, he was looking down on them from above. As he said at the very beginning of this same psalm, "The LORD is my light and my salvation; whom shall I fear?" (Ps. 27:1).

Like David, we too may find ourselves facing a wide array of enemies. As we pointed out earlier, they come at us in the form of circumstances, people, besetting sins, failures, infirmities, the world system, Satan and all his principalities and powers. Psalm 110:2 promised that the Lord will "extend your mighty scepter from Zion" (NIV). He wanted to extend the sphere of Christ's reign through us. Seated with Christ at his right hand, the Lord invites us to rule in the midst of our enemies. God wants us to go on the offensive.

But like David, to do that we must become worshippers. First, we ascend into worship by setting our hearts and minds on things above where Christ is, seated at God's right hand (Col. 3:1–2). Then we descend into battle against our enemies.

Worship is essential because it causes Jesus to get bigger. Not literally, of course, but bigger in our eyes! We see him for who he always is and was and is to come. Then like David, we boldly declare, "The LORD is my light and my salvation; whom shall I fear?" (Ps. 27:1). *And instead of complaining to God about how big our enemies are, we start proclaiming to our enemies how big our God is!*

Ruling in the midst of our enemies begins in worship. We adore first, then attack; we worship as priests, then reign as kings. As the chorus says, "Majesty, worship his majesty . . . . kingdom authority, flows from his throne unto his own; his anthem raise."[3]

Ruling in Strength and in Weakness

But what does going on the offensive, ruling in the midst of our enemies, actually look like in daily living?

Paul prayed that we would know and experience in our lives the outworking of "the immeasurable greatness of [God's] power" (Eph. 1:19). So let's consider two concrete ways it's often played out in our lives.

Ruling through Strength

"You cannot pass!" cried Gandalf the Great in a memorable scene in the *The Fellowship of the Ring*, the first book of J. R. R. Tolkien's *The Lord of the Rings* trilogy. Gandalf declared those courageous, determined words at the Bridge of Khazad-dum, as he turned and blocked the path of a Balrog, a huge, fiery demon that was pursuing the members of the Fellowship of the Ring as they fled from the dark underground complex of Moria. "You cannot pass!" he insisted. "I am a servant of the Secret Fire, wielder of the Flame of Anor . . . The dark fire will not avail you, flame of Udun! Go back to the shadow! You cannot pass!"[4]

Ruling in the midst of our enemies in right-hand-of-God power will sometimes mean—like Gandalf in the face of the Balrog, or David in the face of Goliath—turning and facing our enemies head-on, standing firm, and boldly declaring, "You shall not pass." Unlike Gandalf, you may not consider yourself "a servant of the Secret Fire, [or] wielder of the Flame of Anor," but make no mistake, you too can stand resolute, look your enemies straight in the eye, and remind them of *who* you are and *where* you are in Christ. You too can boldly declare, "I am a beloved daughter or son of the King. I am a servant of the Most High. I am seated with Christ at God's right hand. All authority has been given unto him and he has bestowed his authority and power upon me. Therefore, in Jesus' name I declare, *you shall not pass!*"

Our enemies want to convince us that they wield all the authority and power so we'll be intimidated by them. Think of Gideon, for example. When the angel of the Lord first appeared to him, he was threshing wheat, not outside on an open floor as was customary, but inside a winepress so that he wouldn't be detected by the Midianites, Israel's oppressors.

How shocked he must have been when an angel appeared to him and declared, "The LORD is with you, you mighty warrior. . . . Go in this might of yours and deliver Israel from the hand of Midian" (Judges 6:12–14).

Mighty warrior? Gideon must have wondered who the angel was talking to. "Who? Me?" He was a reluctant warrior at best, a man of little faith who needed lots of convincing. Only after he put out several fleeces and God proved faithful each time would Gideon begin to entertain the notion that it might be true.

Mighty warrior? O, you of little faith! So often, like Gideon, we too are reluctant to believe *who* we are in Christ and *where* we are seated with him. What Oswald Chambers said is so perceptive and true: "There is more hindrance to God's work because people cling to a sense of unworthiness than because of conceit."[5] We cling to a sense of unworthiness, pessimism, and defeat instead of clinging to God's promises. No wonder Paul prayed for us that we might know "the immeasurable greatness of his power for us who believe" (Eph. 1:19).

In the face of certain enemies in your life, in the life of your family, workplace, church, or community, Christ may be saying, "Mighty warrior, rise up. Rule in the midst of your enemies! Shake off your passivity. Stop letting your enemies push you around. Go on the offensive. Stand up and fight. Draw a line in the stand. Look them in the eye and forcefully declare, 'Enough is enough. I refuse to let you do that. You shall not pass! No longer am I a footstool for your feet. It's time for you to become a part of Christ's footstool!'"

When we do that—make no mistake—our enemies won't take it lying down. They will launch a counter-offensive. Often they will use discouragement to push us back and wear us down (Dan. 7:25). That's why we must regularly do what the early Christians did. In the face of the increasing threats and resistance, they gathered together to pray—not so that God would get rid of the opposition, but that their strength and boldness would be renewed and increased. "And now, Lord, look at their threats, and grant to your servants to speak your word with all boldness" (Acts 4:29). We too must pray regularly and consistently, privately and corporately, waiting on the Lord that he might renew our strength (Isa. 40:30–31) and fill us anew with the Spirit, like he did the fledgling church: "When they had prayed, the place in which they were gathered together was shaken;

and they were all filled with the Holy Spirit and spoke the word of God with boldness" (Acts 4:31).

"Rule in the midst of your enemies!" Sometimes it means that in the face of our enemies, even when we feel overwhelmed and outnumbered, we must rise up and fight and, like Gandalf, boldly declare, "You cannot pass!"

Ruling through Weakness

But there is also another way we "take the offensive" in ruling in the midst of our enemies. Because it is counter-intuitive, paradoxical, and stands in such sharp contrast to the way we normally think, many Christians fail to grasp it. We encounter it most clearly and profoundly at the cross, where Christ ultimately and decisively overcomes and defeats God's evil enemies. Yet he rules over them not through passive resignation, brute strength, or a dazzling display of dominating power. Instead he rules through divine weakness and the power of suffering love.

In his first letter to the young church at Corinth, the apostle Paul stated that God's way, revealed in the cross, is so strange and startling that it is "a stumbling block to Jews and foolishness to Gentiles" (1 Cor. 1:23). Nevertheless, it is a demonstration of divine power and wisdom. "For God's foolishness is wiser than human wisdom, and God's weakness is stronger than human strength" (1 Cor. 1:25).

How, then, does what Jesus did through the cross relate to us? What might it say about how we may be called to rule in the midst of our enemies? In his second letter to that same group of Corinthian believers, Paul shared candidly about a thorn in the flesh (2 Cor. 12:7) he had to contend with. It is an instructive example of what ruling in the midst of our enemies through weakness looks like.[6]

Skolops, the Greek word for "thorn," can mean either a stake, which actually pegged a person to the ground or a splinter, which was constantly irritating. According to one biblical commentator, it conveyed "the notion of something sharp and painful which sticks deep in the flesh and in the will of God defies extraction. The effect of its presence was to cripple Paul's enjoyment of life, and to frustrate his full efficiency by draining his energies."[7] There has been much conjecture about the exact nature of Paul's "thorn." Was it a particular person who relentlessly opposed Paul, persecution in general, a besetting sin or temptation, a speech impediment, a physical infirmity such as epilepsy or an eye disorder? All these have been put forward as possibilities, but no one knows for sure. The fact that Paul doesn't specify, however, has meant that Christians have been able to apply what he says to various kinds of thorns in their lives, which they perceive as enemies.

Paul called his thorn "a messenger of Satan to torment me" (12:7). There is no doubt, then, that he viewed it as an enemy, something evil which was intended to thwart God's purposes for him. So at first, he vigorously and persistently prayed for its removal: "Three times I appealed to the Lord about this, that it would leave me" (12:8). His specific mention of praying three times reminds us of how Christ prayed three times in Gethsemane, "If it is possible, let this cup pass from me" (Matt. 26:39).

However, that's not how Paul's prayer was answered. His thorn was *not* taken away. Rather, he heard the Lord say, "My grace is sufficient for you, for power is made perfect in weakness" (12:9). God's response to Paul's thorn was not to remove it, but to give Paul grace to endure, and to use Paul's resulting weakness as an opportunity to demonstrate divine power. Just as Christ himself was "crucified in weakness" (2 Cor. 13:4) and his weakness in death demonstrated the power of God (1 Cor. 1:22–25), Paul's thorn-related weakness produced similar results. In fact, he claimed that God's power is *perfected* in weakness.

No doubt God could have demonstrated his power by removing it. But by not removing it, God chose to do something even better, to perfect his power through weakness. As a result, this transformed Paul's attitude toward his thorn. Instead of its presence signaling a defeat, or fueling anger or self-pity, the weakness caused by the thorn gave him something to boast about. "So, I will boast all the more gladly of my weaknesses," he exclaimed, "so that the power of Christ may dwell in me" (12:9).

Moreover, contrary to what we would think, Paul's thorn-produced weakness didn't create frustration and dissatisfaction in him. Instead it led to contentment. "Therefore I am content with weaknesses," he declared, for he realized that "whenever I am weak, then I am strong" (12:10).

Sometimes, then, this is how we rule in the midst of our enemies—not through boldly standing against them and declaring our authority in Christ, but strangely, through embracing them as friends, receiving God's sufficient grace for them, and allowing God's power to be manifest in us in weakness. Yes, sometimes we rule by even boasting in and being content with our weaknesses, knowing that when we are weak, God's power and his strength can be realized and increase in us.

I wonder what are the enemies in your life that may be like Paul's thorn in the flesh? God's will for your ruling over these particular enemies is not to remove them, nor for you to rise up and overcome them through bold forceful strength. God's will for your ruling is to say, "My grace is sufficient for you. My strength will be made manifest in your weakness."

Concerning a thorn in the flesh in his life, an enemy, which he was called to rule over not through strength but through weakness, Augustine is often attributed with saying this: "In my deepest wound, I saw your glory and it dazzled me."[8] Are there deep wounds in your life that God wants to use as channels of his glory? His light often shines brightest in our brokenness.

Because Jesus is ascended, he is ruling and will continue to rule until all his enemies have become a footstool for his feet. Because we are in Christ and raised up with him, we are invited to rule too. Hear the invitation, then, to "rule in the midst of your enemies." Pray and ask the Lord to help you discern what that might mean in relation to each of the particular enemies in your life. Where are you being called to rise up and rule in authority and strength? Where are you being invited to rule in acceptance and weakness? Regardless of how Christ is calling you to rule, as Paul insisted, "in all these things we are more than conquerors through him" (Rom. 8:37).

Questions for Personal and Group Reflection

1. Enemies can come at us in the form of circumstances, people, besetting sins, failures, infirmities, the world system, Satan, and all his principalities and powers. Where in your life are you most feeling the force of your enemies right now? How might looking down at your enemies, as you are seated with Christ above, affect the way you face them?

2. In the face of our enemies, we first ascend into worship and then descend into war. How and where does worship take place in your life now? How might Christ be calling you to go deeper and grow as a worshipper?

3. Where in your life, and in the face of which of your enemies, is the ascended Christ saying to you, "This

day we fight"? Where is he inviting you to rule in his strength and authority? Where is he encouraging you to rise up and say, "You shall not pass!"?

4. Are there situations in your life, like Paul's thorn in the flesh, where Christ is saying, "I'm not going to take this away, but my strength will be made perfect in weakness"? Where is he calling you to rule, not through strength, but in weakness? What practically do you think that will mean for you?

5. Have there been situations in your life where Christ has worked to bring light out of darkness, to use even your wounds to display his glory? Give him praise and gratitude for what he has done.

CHAPTER SIX

An Intercessory Life

The LORD has sworn and will not change his mind,
"You are a priest forever according to the order of
Melchizedek."

—PSALM 110:4

The LORD says to my lord, 'Sit at my right hand until I make your enemies a footstool for your feet'" (Ps. 110:1 NIV). We keep coming back to this verse cited by the New Testament writers more than any other verse in the Old Testament. It means, as we stressed earlier, that the ascended Christ has been installed and reigns as King forever.

But a few verses later, the same psalm mentions another office into which he has been installed: "The LORD has sworn and will not change his mind, 'You are a priest forever according to the order of Melchizedek'" (Ps. 110:4). So the ascended Christ is not only a King forever, he is also a priest forever. Jesus is our Great High

Priest! And it is the priestly dimension of his work, fore-told in the words of this psalm, that we will focus on in this chapter.

Notice Psalm 110 specifies that he is a priest "according to the order of Melchizedek." Long before God instructed Moses to install Aaron as the first Jewish high priest (Exod. 28), Melchizedek, "priest of the Most High God" showed up. He was a mysterious figure who appeared out of thin air to bless the patriarch Abraham after Abraham had just defeated five Canaanite kings in order to rescue his nephew, Lot (Gen. 14:17–20). Melchizedek received gifts from Abraham and then disappeared, never to be mentioned again until this verse in Psalm 110.

According to the writer of Hebrews, unlike Aaron, Melchizedek became a priest "not by meeting the physical requirement of belonging to the tribe of Levi, but by the power of a life that cannot be destroyed" (Heb. 7:16 NLT). That's why Jesus is a priest "according to the order of Melchizedek," not the order of Aaron. His resurrection and ascension prove that his life is indestructible. He lives forever and his priesthood therefore lasts forever.

Having ascended into heaven to God's right hand, Jesus is now our Great High Priest and is engaged in the work of intercession on our behalf.[1] As Paul declared, "It is Christ Jesus, who died, yes, who was raised, who is at the right hand of God, who indeed intercedes for us" (Rom. 8:34). Likewise, the writer of Hebrews told us that Jesus, our Eternal High Priest, "always lives to make intercession" (Heb. 7:25). In fact, according to Thomas Oden, this is "the principal feature of the heavenly session of Christ," that "he enters into an intercessory ministry for humanity in the presence of the Father, pleading humanity's case before the Father."[2]

In "Arise, My Soul Arise," one of his classic hymns, Charles Wesley described it like this:

> He ever lives above, for me to intercede;
> His all redeeming love, His precious blood to plead . . .
> Five bleeding wounds He bears, received on Calvary.
> They pour effectual prayers; they strongly speak for me.
> "Forgive him, oh, forgive!" they cry, "Nor let that ransomed sinner die."[3]

Recently, another hymn, based on the words of Charitie Lees Bancroft, a nineteenth-century hymnwriter, has been adapted and is being sung in contemporary worship settings. Her words, similar to Wesley's, are helping many Christians today grasp this great ascension truth. The first verse expresses it like this:

> Before the throne of God above
> I have a strong and perfect plea:
> A great High Priest, whose name is Love,
> Who ever lives and pleads for me.
> My name is graven on His hands,
> My name is written on His heart;

I know that while in heaven He stands,
No tongue can bid me thence depart.
No tongue can bid me thence depart.[4]

Both hymns help picture for us the work of intercession the ascended Christ is presently engaged in on our behalf. He stands in the gap for us so that "we have an advocate with the Father, Jesus Christ the righteous" (1 John 2:1). Jesus prays without ceasing for his wayward bride, the church. He cries out on behalf of the lost world, the fallen creation he died to save and redeem.

Moreover, as the writer of Hebrews emphasized, because our Great High Priest understands our weaknesses, his intercession is full of sympathy and compassion (Heb. 4:15). Made of flesh and blood (Heb. 2:14), fully human like us, he has gone through suffering and testing and is able to help us when we are being tried and tested (Heb. 2:18). "It is as our Brother, wearing our humanity," theologian T. F. Torrance reminded us, "that He has ascended presenting Himself eternally before the face of the Father, and presenting us in Himself."[5]

His intercession for us is also intensely personal. Aaron, the Old Testament high priest, wore a chest piece containing twelve gemstones, one for each of Israel's twelve tribes, in order to "bear the names" of the tribes "on his heart" as he entered into the Lord's presence (Exod. 28:29). Likewise, Jesus, our Great High Priest, holds each of us near and dear to his heart as he presents us to the Father. Each one of our names is truly written on his hands and graven on his heart. Knowing that Jesus is praying for us, particularly when we are in the midst of suffering and difficulty, can truly be a great source of gratitude, confidence, and joy.

Joining with Christ in the Work of Intercession

If, then, the ascended Christ is now engaged in this high priestly work of intercession on our behalf and on behalf of the world, it stands to reason that we too, having been raised up and seated with him (Eph. 2:6), will also find ourselves joining him in that work. As we "set our minds on things above" (Col. 3:2), we will be drawn into his work of intercession, assuming a priestly, standing-in-the-gap posture for others.

But what might that look like in our lives? And what might characterize the intercession to which we may be called, particularly in the realm of prayer? To answer those questions, I want to share a personal experience where the reality of intercession—both Christ's and mine—came home to me in an unforgettable, life-changing way. Then I want to discuss what I've been learning in the school of intercession as a result.

In May 1990, I was in Ypsilanti, Michigan, on the campus of Eastern Michigan University, attending a conference for pastors and Christian leaders. Fifteen hundred people were gathered in the gymnasium on the first evening of the conference for a time of extended worship and ministry. John Wimber from the Vineyard Christian Fellowship was leading the service. After he had preached, scores of people responded to his invitation. When they had gathered at the front, Wimber began to pray over them.

I was sitting between my father and a close friend, intently observing what was happening, sensing the Holy Spirit's presence in our midst. Then suddenly, John Wimber prayed with authority: "Lord, let the spirit of intercession fall upon your people now." Up until then the furthest thing from my mind was Asbury Theological Seminary where I teach. In fact, one of my reasons for attending the conference was to *get away* from the seminary and the end-of-semester busyness. But as soon as John Wimber spoke those words, I found myself thinking about the seminary and especially about the bitter conflict over a particular issue that had deeply divided our faculty for several years.

Before I knew it, there were tears in my eyes. I wasn't just thinking about the situation, I was *crying* about it. Then I found myself not just crying, but *crying out* so loudly that everyone seated around me could hear me. There was such a deep groaning within me that I couldn't contain myself: "Oh, God!" I kept crying, "Oh, God!" And I couldn't stop. My stomach was contracting as if I were vomiting. The groaning and the crying went on for several minutes.

When I finally quieted down, the Lord seemed to whisper to me, "I know the conflict at the seminary has been troubling and upsetting to you, but you have no idea what it's been doing to me. It's breaking my heart, Steve. It's breaking my heart."

A few days after I returned from the conference, I was talking with several faculty colleagues. They were expressing their concern about a faculty meeting I had missed while attending the conference. During that meeting the underlying conflict and division had erupted again. I took a deep breath and said, "Can I tell you about something that happened to me a few days ago?" Then with considerable hesitation, not sure of what they would think of my strange, "off-the-wall" experience, I described what had happened to me that evening at the conference. When I had finished, my colleagues seemed to be taken aback. "Since I've returned from that conference," I told them, "God has placed a burden on my heart as never before simply to pray for our situation. Would you like to join with me sometime next week for a time of intercessory prayer for the seminary?"

They all agreed. So a few days later we got together—about seven of us—and for more than an hour we prayed. We didn't analyze the problem or propose solutions—something we seminary professors are so prone to do. We simply prayed. Like King Jehoshaphat in the face of the vast enemy army, we were at the point where all we could say was, "We do not know what to do, but our eyes are on you" (2 Chron. 20:12).

Over the summer months, I personally went to many other faculty members, told them about my experience, and invited them to what became a monthly faculty intercessory prayer meeting that continued for the next year and a half. In the fall of that same year, during a faculty meeting, we witnessed a major breakthrough over the conflict that had torn and divided us. After that meeting there was a noticeable shift and our community began to heal.

Since that time, intercessory prayer, where the focus of our praying is on others and not ourselves, has taken on a meaning and importance it never had before. In many ways, that experience marked my initiation into the school of intercession. Here, then, are some of the lessons I am learning about Christ's ascension work of intercession and our joining with him. My prayer is that what I have learned might be helpful to you.

Intercession as Participation

Christ, our Great High Priest is always the principal actor in intercession. As the church father Ambrose insisted, "Unless He intercedes there is no intercourse with God either for us or for all saints."[6] Our intercession, then, is simply a participation in the ongoing intercession of the ascended Christ.

It is so important to grasp this. It means that ultimately the burden of intercession is not *ours*, but *his*. We are therefore never called to bear the burden of intercession alone, but to piggyback on Christ's intercession, to be co-laborers with him, through the Holy Spirit (Rom. 8:26–27) in his ongoing intercession in heaven.

What I experienced that evening in Michigan brought this truth home to me in a powerful, dramatic way. In reflecting on what happened, I realized that as I cried out, I was caught up in something much bigger than I was and something I hadn't initiated. For just a few moments I had experienced, in a small measure, something of the depth and intensity of Christ's intercession. In some mysterious way, I believe I was caught up in the intercession of the Son at the Father's right hand.

Of course, I don't usually experience the reality of the ascended Christ's intercession in such a dramatic fashion. Often when I intercede for others, I *feel* very little. But that doesn't discourage me as it once might have. Realizing that my intercession is a participation in Christ's intercession, I find myself simply inviting Jesus to pray in and through me for that particular person or situation. I also invite the Holy Spirit to join me to Christ and to come as the spirit of intercession to show me how to pray for others and to pray in me on their behalf. And he does! As Paul reminded us, "the Spirit helps us in our weakness; for we do not know how to pray as we ought, but that very Spirit intercedes with sighs too deep for words" (Rom. 8:26).

Sometimes, however, we forget this and we mistakenly take the burden of intercession on ourselves—as if somehow it depends on us or we have to "make it happen." Then we feel guilty when our passion and fervor subsides or we fail to pray for others the way we know we should. So we need to remind ourselves that our intercession, as significant as it is, is always secondary to Christ's. When we realize we are called to intercede *with* him rather than *for* him, then we discover that his yoke is easy and his burden is light (Matt. 11:29).

Early in her ministry, Amy Carmichael (1867–1951), who spent more than fifty years as a missionary in south India, was given a deep burden for young girls who were dedicated to the Hindu gods and given to temple priests to earn money through prostitution. But as she began to expose this practice and take action in seeking to rescue these temple children, there came a point when the opposition—both human and demonic—became so intense she was ready to give up. Even some of her fellow missionaries stood against her. "You can't 'rock the boat' like this," they warned. "If you keep it up, the government authorities will make us all leave."

As a result, Amy was ready to give up. "Lord," she cried, "this burden you've put on my heart for these girls—I can't carry it anymore." Then one day she came to realize whose burden it really was. Here's how she describes it:

> At last a day came when the burden grew too heavy for me; and then it was as though the tamarind trees about the house were not tamarind, but olive, and under one of these trees our

Lord Jesus knelt alone. And I knew that this was His burden, not mine. It was He who was asking me to share it with Him, not I who was asking Him to share it with me. After that there was only one thing to do; who, after seeing Him kneeling there, could turn away and forget? Who could have done anything but go into the garden and kneel down beside Him under the olive trees?[7]

The ascended Christ is looking for those who will join him in his great high priestly work. Seated with him at God's right hand, we are called to *participate* in the work that he is doing, not *initiate* the work or take the burden on ourselves. Realizing this changes our attitude toward intercession.

Intercession as Identification

As we said earlier, the ascended Christ who intercedes for us is one who fully identifies with us in our humanity. He became flesh and blood, shared in our weakness, and experienced temptation. He even bore our sins in his body on the cross (1 Peter 2:24) and, though he knew no sin, he was made sin for us (2 Cor. 5:21). Because Christ goes to such great lengths to identify with those for whom he intercedes, we too, when we join with him in his intercession, will also find ourselves joined to those with whom we are called to intercede. We will identify ourselves with them to the point where we are willing to confess their sins on their behalf and even acknowledge the extent to which we have participated in those sins ourselves.

Like Nehemiah did, for example, when he heard the news that the walls and gates of Jerusalem were in ruins. He "sat down and wept" and for days he "mourned and fasted and prayed" (Neh. 1:4). Although Nehemiah was indeed a righteous man, in his prayer of confession he acknowledges the sins of his people as if they were his own: "I confess the sins we Israelites, including myself and my father's family, have committed against you. We have acted very wickedly toward you" (Neh. 1:6–7 NIV).

Similarly, Daniel also pleaded with God on behalf of the people "in prayer and petition, in fasting, and in sackcloth and ashes" (Dan. 9:3 NIV). Few were more righteous than Daniel, yet he prayed, "We have sinned and done wrong. We have been wicked and have rebelled" (Dan. 9:5 NIV). Both these great intercessors identified themselves with the people they were praying for. They not only prayed, "Lord, forgive *them*." They prayed, "Lord, forgive *us*."

Following my experience at the conference when God placed a burden upon my heart for the deep conflict at the seminary, I often found myself doing the same thing. I could no longer point my finger at other members of the faculty and self-righteously blame them for our problems. I saw, as never before, that the very attitudes I despised in others were lodged in my own heart as well. At one prayer meeting in particular, I suddenly found myself weeping and confessing the sins of the seminary on behalf of the seminary, even while I confessed them as my own sins.

Several years later something similar happened when I was praying for one of my teenage sons. He had said, in relation to some who were in authority over him, "I'll submit to them outwardly, but I'll never do it from the heart." His attitude saddened and disturbed me, and so I began to pray that God would change his heart.

But one day as I was praying for him, the Lord said to me, "Where do you think he learned that attitude? Like father, like son! You do the very same thing in relation to certain people in your life. Outwardly, you smile and are agreeable with them, but inwardly, your heart is seething with anger and rebellion. Before I change that attitude in your son, I first want to change it in you."

Intercession sometimes leads to such deep identification. Our prayers to change others may cause us to change too!

Intercession as Sacrifice

In the hymn "Arise, My Soul, Arise," Charles Wesley's poetic description of Christ, our Great High Priest, conveys that his intercession is intense, persistent, costly, and sacrificial:

> Five bleeding wounds He bears, received on
> Calvary.
> They pour effectual prayers; they strongly plead
> for me.

"Forgive him, oh, forgive!" they cry . . . "Nor let
that ransomed sinner die!"[8]

If we join in prayer with Jesus, our Great High Priest,
we may be led to such persistent, costly intercession as
well. At daybreak, Jacob tenaciously clung to the angel he
had wrestled with all night and cried, "I will not let you
go, unless you bless me" (Gen. 32:26). An intercessor, one
who stands in the gap, is like that. Except intercessors
don't cry, "I will not let you go until you bless *me*," but
"I will not let you go until you bless *them*"—that family
member, or relative, or friend, or congregation, or age-
group, or people-group, or city, or nation, or whatever it
is Jesus seems to have laid upon their heart.

Intercessors stand in the gap for others, pleading
to God on their behalf. "Lord, have mercy on them,"
they implore. "Don't hold it against them. Change their
hearts. Cause them to turn to you."

Like Jacob, intercessors are stubborn and persistent.
"Lord, I'm not going anywhere," they pray. "I am digging
in my heels. I will stay here until this situation is resolved
. . . until this person comes to know you . . . until this
congregation is renewed . . . until the church is planted
. . . until that unreached people-group hears the gospel.
Lord, I will not let you go until you bless them."

And make no mistake, joining with Christ in intercession for others is costly business. In fact, Oswald
Chambers maintained that this is the primary way in
which we participate in Christ's sufferings.[9] We may

find ourselves distraught over some person or situation, agonizing in prayer over it; at times even, like Nehemiah and Daniel mentioned above, being led to fast on account of it.

That's what happened to me the summer following my experience at the conference in Michigan. I knew there were numerous references in the Bible that commended fasting. As a United Methodist pastor, I also knew what an important part fasting had played in the life of John Wesley and the early Methodists. When I was ordained, I had affirmed the nineteen historic questions that Wesley had put to his lay preachers. The sixteenth question reads, "Will you recommend fasting and abstinence, both by precept and example?" Yet, I must confess, I had never done either.

During the summer after the conference, that changed. I was moved to fast not only on account of myself and my own spiritual life, but also on behalf of the seminary. Since that time, as I've been impressed to pray for persons and situations, sometimes God puts within me a desire to fast for them. I don't understand exactly how it works, but I believe that when we are willing to identify with others even to the point of sacrificing on their behalf (whether through fasting or some other means), God's presence and power is released in greater measure in their lives and circumstances.

As we open ourselves to the Spirit of Christ and identify with others, we are drawn in toward suffering and sacrifice on their behalf. And much to our own

amazement—knowing how self-centered we tend to be—
we finding ourselves joyfully engaging in this form of
redemptive suffering.

A few years before his death, Baron Friedrich
Von Hügel (1852–1925), the great spiritual director and
writer, wrote in a letter to his niece about his years of
faithful intercession (often in the wee hours of the night)
on behalf of one of his daughters:

> I wonder whether you realize a deep, great fact?
> That souls—all human souls—are deeply intercon-
> nected? That, I mean, we cannot only pray for each
> other, but suffer for each other? That these long,
> trying wakings, that I was able to offer them to
> God and to Christ for my [child]—that He might
> ever strengthen, sweeten, steady her in her true,
> simple, humble love and dependence upon Him.
> Nothing is more real than this inter-connection—
> this gracious power put by God Himself into the
> very heart of our infirmities.[10]

Such intercessory prayer grows out of our union
with the ascended Christ in his work of intercession.
Paul informed the Colossian believers that Epaphras
was praying that way for them. "He is always wrestling in
prayer for you, that you may stand firm in all the will of
God, mature and fully assured" (Col. 4:12 NIV). We may
be called to such sacrificial prayer wrestling on behalf of
others as well.

Intercession as Battle

Like it or not, all Christians are engaged in spiritual warfare—a violent battle with Satan in which we seek to reclaim enemy territory that rightfully belongs to Christ. As it did for Epaphras, prayer can involve wrestling. For, as Paul reminded us, "our struggle is not against flesh and blood," but against "the powers of this dark world" and "the spiritual forces of evil in the heavenly realms" (Eph. 6:12 NIV). Intercessory prayer is our *primary* offensive weapon. Engage in it with any degree of seriousness and you will soon find yourself in the heat of the battle.

Our ascended King Jesus, and Great High Priest, is engaged in it too! Ever since he sat down at the right hand of God, the writer of Hebrews tells us, echoing Psalm 110:1 again, he "has been waiting 'until his enemies would be made a footstool for his feet'" (Heb. 10:13). As he waits, he wrestles in prayer on our behalf. He intercedes on behalf of the church and the world. When we join him in his intercession, we wrestle with him as he fights against his enemies.

From the world's point of view, intercessory prayer appears weak and ineffective. If you want to change a person or situation, doesn't it make more sense to take a direct, hands-on approach? But as Paul pointed out, the weapons of our warfare are spiritual, not worldly. They have divine power to demolish strongholds and to take every thought captive to make it obedient to Christ (2 Cor. 10:3–6).

Nonetheless, Christ's enemies are stubborn and resistant. They submit and yield territory only when they are forced to. So as we engage in the battle of intercession, we must be patient and persistent. Often, as we pray for persons or situations, there is no apparent change in them. Sometimes they even seem to get worse! After a while it is easy to stop praying. But if we keep praying for them on the basis of faith in what the Spirit of God is doing, eventually it begins to make a difference.

I have been challenged and encouraged as I engage in the battle of intercession for others by a statement of Oswald Chambers:

> When we pray for others the Spirit of God works in the unconscious domain of their being which we know nothing about, and the one we are praying for knows nothing about . . . We may have spoken until we are worn out, but have never come anywhere near, and we have given up in despair. But if we have been praying, we find on meeting them one day that there is the beginning of a softening in an inquiry and a desire to know something. It is that kind of intercession that does most damage to Satan's kingdom.[11]

We must not lose heart, and we must persevere in prayer in spite of what we see. In another of his wonderful hymns, "Soldiers of Christ, Arise," Charles Wesley encourages us in the battle with these words: "From strength to strength go on. Wrestle and fight and pray. Tread all the powers of darkness down. And win the well-fought day."[12]

As we patiently engage in the battle of intercessory prayer through the power of the Holy Spirit, slowly, but surely and amazingly, God works. Yes, little by little, Christ's enemies are being made into a footstool for his feet.

These are the lessons I've been learning about joining with Jesus, our ascended Lord and Great High Priest, in his work of intercession. What have you been learning? What burdens for intercession has God placed on your heart? Who has he called you to pray for? Above all, I trust you are discovering in your life what I continue to discover in mine: When we *intercede*, Christ *intervenes*!

Questions for Personal and Group Reflection

1. What has been your experience with intercessory prayer? Have you known people who you consider to be prayer warriors? Were there those who especially prayed that you would give your life to Christ? Have you been led at times to especially pray for certain people or situations?

2. Jesus is our Great High Priest who intercedes for us. What does this biblical truth convey to you? How does it make you think and feel about Jesus?

3. The ascended Christ is looking for those who will join him in his great high priestly work. Seated with him at God's right hand, we are called to *participate* in the work that he is doing, not *initiate* the work or take the burden on ourselves. Why is properly understanding the division of labor—Christ's part and ours in the work of intercession—so important? Have you ever failed to grasp it rightly? What happened as a result?

4. Have you ever found yourself having to deal with attitudes in yourself as you prayed for persons and situations the Lord had led you to pray for? How have you been changed as you prayed for God to change others?

5. How have you experienced the costliness of intercession in your life?

6. What has been your experience with fasting?

7. How have you experienced spiritual battle in the context of intercession?

CHAPTER SEVEN

Mission Possible

"All authority in heaven and on earth has been given to me. Go therefore and make disciples of all nations, baptizing them in the name of the Father and of the Son and of the Holy Spirit, and teaching them to obey everything that I have commanded you. And remember, I am with you always, to the end of the age."

—MATTHEW 28:18–20

"But you will receive power when the Holy Spirit has come upon you; and you will be my witnesses in Jerusalem, in all Judea and Samaria, and to the ends of the earth." When he had said this, as they were watching, he was lifted up, and a cloud took him out of their sight.

—ACTS 1:8–9

When I think about the biblical basis for Christian mission, the words of Jesus in the two passages above come immediately to mind. In the first, at the end of Matthew and commonly known as the Great Commission, the risen Christ commanded his disciples to "go make disciples of all nations." In the second, at the beginning of Acts, Jesus told his disciples that they will receive the power of the Holy Spirit and will be his witnesses "to the ends of the earth." For years, these two passages—the Great Commission and the promise of the Holy Spirit—have stood as foundational pillars in undergirding my understanding of the basis for our mission to go into all the world with the gospel of Christ.

Until recently, however, I never grasped the relationship between these pillars and the ascension of Christ. Both of them, in fact, rest firmly upon it. Without his ascension there would be no Great Commission and no promise of the Spirit. It is the basis for both our being sent to make disciples and the Holy Spirit being sent to empower us as witnesses. Mission is possible because of the ascension.

The Ascension and the Great Commission

Look closely at the Great Commission again. Notice before the command to "go make disciples," Jesus emphatically declared, "All authority in heaven and on earth has been given to me." In fact, that declaration is the reason we are told to "go make disciples"—because all authority has been given to him.

And when was all authority given to Jesus? It was, as Paul said, "when [God] raised him from the dead and *seated him at his right hand in the heavenly places*, far above all rule and authority and power and dominion . . . [and] put all things under his feet" (Eph. 1:20–22, italics mine).

It is when Christ ascends that all authority—the authority that is the basis for our going to make disciples—is conferred upon him. In chapter 5, we considered what Christ's ascension and authority means for us in relation to our enemies. Because of his ascension and authority, and our position seated with Christ in the heavenly realms, we emphasized that we can be "more than conquerors" and, in fact, "rule in the midst of our enemies." In this chapter, we want to focus on another important aspect of his ascension and authority. It is the basis for our going into all the world to make disciples. As Ben Patterson put it, "the great commission is grounded in the authority of Christ's ascension."[1]

Like Psalm 110, the psalm we have repeatedly come back to throughout this book, the New Testament writers also understood Psalm 2 as a messianic psalm fulfilled by the risen, ascended Christ. According to that psalm, though the nations rage and the rulers of this world conspire "against the LORD and his anointed" (Ps. 2:2), God who sits in heaven laughs and emphatically declares, "I have set my king on Zion, my holy hill" (Ps. 2:6). And to his anointed king the Lord says, "You are my son; today I have begotten you. *Ask of me, and I will make the nations your heritage, and the ends of the earth your possession*" (Ps. 2:7–8, italics mine).

The nations, then, have been given by the Father to the Son as an inheritance and a possession. Echoing Psalm 2, and on the basis of his authority over the nations, the ascended Christ says to the church, "To everyone who conquers and continues to do my works to the end, I will give authority over the nations . . . even as I also received authority from my Father" (Rev. 2:26–28).

Accordingly, Christ's command that we make disciples of all nations flows from the authority he received when he ascended to the Father's right hand. "All power and authority in heaven and on earth has been given to me" (Matt. 28:18). This means that the power and authority to carry out the work of redemption and bring it to consummation in every nation has been placed in the hands of the risen, ascended Christ!

Do you see, then, how the Great Commission is grounded in the authority bestowed upon Christ through the ascension? And, as if that weren't enough, there's more! After Jesus commissions them to make disciples in every nation, he immediately adds, "And remember, I am with you always, to the end of the age" (Matt. 28:20). Jesus promises that wherever they go, they will never be alone. He will always be with them.

And it's because of his ascension into heaven that he can make that promise. As we emphasized earlier, because he is in heaven, he can now "fill all things" (Eph. 4:10). That means Christ can now be personally present, not just in one place at one time, as during his earthly life, but *in all places at all times.* Through the Holy Spirit, the ascended

Jesus, who is in heaven, is here now with us on earth, in person, every moment, every day, everywhere.

So his authority ("All authority has been given to me") and his presence ("I am with you always")—are *both* grounded in the ascension. They are like bookends, holding up the Great Commission ("Go make disciples of all nations"), which is sandwiched in between. But without the ascension there are no bookends and without the bookends the Great Commission collapses.

The Ascension and the Outpouring of the Holy Spirit

Having established the connection between the ascension and the Great Commission, now let's consider the connection between the ascension and the promise of the Holy Spirit. Notice there is a close connection right in the text. Here is Acts 1:8–9 again: "'But you will receive power when the Holy Spirit has come upon you; and you will be my witnesses in Jerusalem, in all Judea and Samaria, and to the ends of the earth.' When he had said this, as they were watching, he was lifted up, and a cloud took him out of their sight."

Immediately after Jesus promises that they will receive power to be his witnesses through the power of the Holy Spirit, he ascends into heaven! Luke, the writer of Acts, wants us to understand that the Holy Spirit couldn't descend until Jesus ascends. So he is careful to emphasize that "when he had said this" (i.e., about the

Spirit's coming on them), "he was lifted up." He also closely links Jesus' ascension and the Spirit's coming at the end of his gospel. Immediately after the risen Christ declared, "I am sending upon you what my Father promised," so you will be "clothed with power from on high" (Luke 24:49), he blessed them and ascended into heaven (Luke 24:51).

Earlier in his ministry, Jesus described the coming fullness of the Holy Spirit in terms of "rivers of living water" flowing out of the believer's heart. But John the gospel writer was quick to interject that when Jesus said this, the Spirit had not yet been given, "because Jesus was not yet glorified" (John 7:38–39). That would happen only after Christ's death, resurrection, and ascension. And so, in fact, it did. Ten days after his ascension, on the day of Pentecost, what the prophet Joel prophesied came to pass. The Holy Spirit was poured out on "all flesh" (Joel 2:28–21; Acts 2:1–4, 16–21).

When Peter preached that day and explained to the gathered crowd in Jerusalem what had happened, he was even more explicit in linking the outpouring of the Spirit with Christ's ascension. Some, in fact, maintain that "the climax of Peter's Pentecost sermon is an exposition of the ascension."[2] As Peter declared, "This Jesus God raised up, and of that all of us are witnesses. Being therefore exalted at the right hand of God, and having received from the Father the promise of the Holy Spirit, he has poured out this that you both see and hear" (Acts 2:32–33). Then he immediately went on to quote—you guessed it!—Psalm

110:1: "The Lord said to my Lord, 'Sit at my right hand until I make your enemies a footstool for your feet'" (Acts 2:34–35 NIV).

Because Jesus is ascended, exalted, and enthroned, Peter was saying the promised gift of the Spirit is now ours. In fact, it is the ascended Christ who baptizes us with the Holy Spirit as John the Baptist predicted (Matt. 3:11; Mark 1:8; Luke 3:16; John 1:33).

Consider for a moment all that this means. Through the Spirit, both in our personal lives and as communities of faith, we are given power to be his witnesses (Acts 1:8), to carry out the mission of Christ (John 20:21–22), to live victoriously over sin (Rom. 8:9; Gal. 5:16–25), to overcome weakness (Rom. 8:26), to forgive our enemies (Acts 7:55–60), to know we are God's beloved (Rom. 1:7; 8:15–16), to be bold and courageous (Acts 4:8–13, 29–31), to exercise spiritual authority in Christ (Acts 16:18), to persevere in prayer (Eph. 6:18), and to patiently endure in our weakness and suffering (Rom. 8:22–28).

It is important, then, not to lose sight of this close connection in the New Testament between Christ's ascension and the work of the Holy Spirit. In addition to Peter's sermon, think for example how Paul linked the bestowing of the gifts of the Holy Spirit on the church with Christ's ascension by quoting Psalm 68:18: "When he ascended on high he made captivity itself a captive; he gave gifts to his people" (Eph. 4:8). Too often we separate the Holy Spirit from the ascended Christ. Although they are not the same and need to be distinguished, there is a unique and inseparable relation between them. In the New Testament the Holy Spirit is sometimes even called the Spirit of Christ (Acts 16:7; Gal. 4:6; 1 Peter 1:11).

In the gospel of John, the close relationship was emphasized by the unique name—*Paraclete*—that Jesus used in reference to the Holy Spirit. No English word is quite comprehensive enough to grasp the full meaning of that Greek word. Biblical scholars do the best they can using various words in our English versions ("Comforter," "Advocate," "Counselor," "Helper") to translate it.

There's no doubt the Paraclete is *distinct* from Jesus himself. Though I am going away, says Jesus, the Paraclete who is "another" is coming to be with you forever (John 14:16). At the same time, the Paraclete is also almost *inseparable* from Jesus.

For example, Jesus told his disciples, "When the [Paraclete] comes, whom I will send to you from the Father . . . he will testify on my behalf" (John 15:26). Later he also said, "He [the Paraclete] will glorify me, because he will take what is mine and declare it to you" (John 16:14). And earlier he insisted, "This is the Spirit of truth . . . You know him, because he abides with you, and he will be in you. 'I will not leave you orphaned; I am coming to you'" (John 14:17–18).

New Testament scholar Raymond Brown included a meticulous ten-page study on the meaning of Paraclete in his two-volume commentary on the gospel of John. Here's what he concluded: when Jesus calls the Holy Spirit the Paraclete, he means "the Holy Spirit in a special role, namely, as *the personal presence of Jesus in the Christian while Jesus is with the Father*"[3] (italics mine).

Through the Paraclete, then, we are connected with our ascended Lord. Jesus is *both* in heaven at the right hand of the Father and through the Holy Spirit personally present in us! In considering what happened on the day of Pentecost, we can easily get preoccupied with the wind, fire, and speaking in tongues—the three external signs present when the Holy Spirit was poured out upon those gathered in the Upper Room (Acts 2:1–4). But above all, when the Holy Spirit was poured out upon the disciples, the personal presence of the risen, ascended Jesus came to dwell in them and abide with them.

G. Campbell Morgan, the great Bible expositor, said it well:

> Then what was new as the result of the coming of the Spirit? Comprehensively, by that whelming of the Spirit, these [men and women], disciples, friends, servants . . . were made actually, though mystically, one with Him in the very fact of His own life. They were made sharers of the life of the Christ. They had never been that before. . . .
>
> When the Spirit came, His actual life passed into their lives . . . In half an hour after Pentecost they knew more about Jesus Christ than they had ever known before. . . .
>
> Were they no longer His servants? Surely His servants, but no longer sent from Him, but the

very instruments of His own going. Their hands became His hands to touch [others] tenderly; their feet, His feet to run on swift errands of God's love; their eyes, His eyes to flame with His tenderness; themselves part of Himself.[4]

When the Holy Spirit came upon them, Jesus himself—the risen, ascended Jesus, seated at the Father's right hand—came alive in them. No longer were they merely sent on a mission by him. Rather, as Morgan put it, they became "the very instruments of His own going." Through the Holy Spirit, Jesus himself, risen and ascended, was now carrying out his mission through them.

Mission in the Power of the Spirit

Consider what this means. We are not the primary actors in mission—Jesus is! Mission is, therefore, not essentially about you and me, working hard, striving to do our best to fulfill the Great Commission, pleading with Jesus to help us in our efforts. Whenever it becomes that, it becomes a heavy yoke, far too much for us to bear. Despite all our best intentions and efforts, our training, our skills, and our strategies, it will end in failure.

How could it be otherwise? We are trying to do something we were never designed to do. Jesus said, "I am the vine, you are the branches" (John 15:5). No matter how hard we try, we can never reverse that! He will always be the vine. We will always be branches. Through our own efforts we may be able to be productive according to human standards. But we will never be fruitful according to God's. "Apart from me," said Jesus, "you can do nothing" (John 15:5). It is the Paraclete, the Holy Spirit, who joins us to the risen, ascended Christ so that he himself can accomplish his mission through us.

Apart from the Spirit's work in us of connecting us to Christ, we will always fail, as Samuel Chadwick wisely observed, "at the point of self-confidence."[5] When we try to go into all the world on our own and in our own strength, we will fail to overcome our own inner fears and inhibitions, to say nothing of the other formidable outward obstacles to mission. Jesus said we would be his witnesses *when* the Holy Spirit comes upon us (Acts 1:8). Yes, and *only when* the Holy Spirit comes upon us!

In the Wesleyan tradition, we often make much of John Wesley's experience at Aldersgate on May 24, 1738, when he "felt his heart strangely warmed." As he recorded in his *Journal*, "I felt I did trust in Christ, Christ alone for salvation; and an assurance was given me that He had taken away my sins, even mine, and saved me from the law of sin and death."[6] And no doubt, had there been no Aldersgate, where Wesley himself came to a deep assurance of his own personal salvation, there surely would have been no ensuing Methodist movement.

But there was also another crucial experience John Wesley had a few months later. In fact, it was actually this experience (when Wesley, along with his brother, Charles, his friend George Whitfield, and around sixty others, experienced an extraordinary outpouring of the Holy Spirit) that really launched John Wesley and the Methodist movement. It happened on New Year's Day, 1739. As members of the Fetter Lane Society, they were all gathered together in the evening for a "love feast" service. Wesley described what happened like this: "About three o'clock in the morning, as we were continuing instant in prayer, the power of God came mightily upon us, insomuch that many cried out for exceeding joy, and many fell to the ground. As soon as we were recovered a little from that awe and amazement at the presence of His Majesty, we broke out with one voice, 'We praise Thee, O God; we acknowledge Thee to be the Lord.'"[7]

This outpouring of the Holy Spirit, of which Wesley said, "the power of God came mightily upon us," catapulted Wesley outward and caused him, and the others there, to become other-directed as never before. Up until then, Wesley had been absorbed in his own quest for personal salvation. What happened at Aldersgate gave him deep assurance about that. Now at Fetter Lane, he was thrust out beyond himself, and the salvation of others became his burning passion.

The clearest indication of this transformation and shift was his embarrassing descent into field preaching four months later. George Whitfield, because of his encounter with the Holy Spirit at the Fetter Lane service, had already begun preaching outdoors in late February. He was amazed at the positive response of the unchurched and the profound way God was working through that unconventional approach to evangelism. He told Wesley about it and urged him to follow suit.

But everything in John Wesley—his church background, his ministerial training, his personality type—cried, No! He was an ordained Anglican priest and an instructor at Oxford who firmly believed all things should be done decently and in order. Preaching was therefore only to happen inside a church and from behind a pulpit. Some in the Church of England maintained that preaching outdoors, or field preaching as it was called, was a violation of civil and canon law.

Wesley himself was certainly not well suited for it. As to personal preference, he was finicky about his personal appearance. He always dressed as neat as a pin and wouldn't tolerate dirt on his clothing. An introvert at heart, he preferred the quiet of a library to the commotion and noise of an unruly crowd.

However, because of the late-night outpouring of the Spirit at Fetter Lane, Wesley was thrust out of himself. Despite all his reservations, he could no longer hold back. On April 2, he crossed the Rubicon. He records what happened in his *Journal*:

> At four in the afternoon I submitted to be more vile and proclaimed in the highways the glad tidings of salvation, speaking from a little eminence in the round adjoining to the city to about three thousand people. The scripture on which I spoke was this, . . . "The Spirit of the

Lord is upon me, because he hath anointed me
to preach the gospel to the poor."[8]

When Wesley said he "submitted to be more vile,"
he really meant it! And from what he said years later we
know that he never really liked field preaching. But when
the Spirit of the Lord comes upon you like it came upon
Wesley and the others that night at Fetter Lane, then as
Jesus said, you *will* be my witnesses and boldly proclaim
everywhere the glad tidings of salvation.

John Wesley became such a Spirit-empowered witness.
In fact, for the next fifty years he preached all over England
in the open air. He traveled some 225,000 miles on horse-
back, preached 40,000 sermons, won as many as 144,000
converts to Christ, and established a vast network of
Methodist societies within the Anglican Church.

Wesley was severely criticized, even by family
members, for field preaching. Anglican Church leaders
reprimanded him because he would not respect the
established boundaries of parishes. But to no avail. In
a famous letter to James Harvey, he explained why he
found it necessary to invade the parishes of other clergy:

> Man forbids me to do this in another's parish:
> that is, in effect, to do it at all; seeing I have now
> no parish of my own, nor probably ever shall.
> Whom, then, shall I hear, God or man? . . . Suffer
> me now to tell you my principles in this matter.
> I look upon all the world as my parish; thus far
> I mean, that in whatever part of it I am, I judge

it meet, right, and my bounden duty to declare, unto all who are willing to hear, the glad tidings of salvation.[9]

Yes, when the Spirit comes upon us, as the Spirit came upon John Wesley, then the whole world becomes our parish. It will be our "bounden duty to declare . . . the glad tidings of salvation." We *will* be witnesses, as Jesus said, in Jerusalem and Judea (our immediate surroundings), in Samaria (across cultures), and to the ends of the earth (all over the globe). Through the Holy Spirit, the risen, ascended Jesus himself will accomplish his mission in the world through us. As G. Campbell Morgan said, we will become "the very instruments of His own going."

Be Filled with the Spirit

No matter who we are, mission can happen through us because Jesus has ascended to the Father. Because he ascended and is enthroned, all authority has been given to him. And because he ascended into heaven, he is not limited by space and time; he is everywhere, always, personally present with us. Furthermore, because he has ascended, he sends the Holy Spirit to indwell us, joining us to himself, to his authority and his presence, so that we can be his witnesses and make disciples of all nations.

Every Christian has been invited to join Christ in his mission and be involved in his Great Commission to "go make disciples." He has called us to be his witnesses in our homes, workplaces, communities, churches, societies, cultures, and nations. What then is the mission Jesus desires to accomplish through you? What does fulfilling the Great Commission mean in your life? Where is your mission field?

We often assume that will mean doing heroic, extraordinary things for Christ. The truth is, in making disciples and being his witnesses, most of us are called to do ordinary things in ordinary places with ordinary people. We are not called, however, to do them in ordinary ways. We are called to do ordinary things in extraordinary ways! And it's because of the ascended Christ himself, his authority and his presence, working through us, that ordinary people like us can do extraordinary things.

As we've emphasized already, Jesus told the disciples that would only happen "when the Holy Spirit has come upon you" (Acts 1:8). So just before he ascended, he promised he would be "sending upon [them] what [his] Father promised" (Luke 24:49). And in his final instructions he told them to "stay here in the city [Jerusalem] until you have been clothed with power from on high" (Luke 24:49).

The disciples took his instructions to heart. Their recent failures in abandoning and denying Jesus made them painfully aware of their inadequacies. So this time they did exactly what he said. After Jesus ascended, they went back to the upstairs room in Jerusalem where they were staying, and for the next ten days, along with "certain women, including Mary the mother of Jesus, as well as [Jesus'] brothers," they "constantly [devoted] themselves to prayer" (Acts 1:14). And then on the day of Pentecost, the ascended Christ fulfilled his promise. The Holy Spirit was poured out upon them (Acts 2:1–4).

I believe the ascended Christ wants to send the Holy Spirit upon you so that together with him you can accomplish his mission. But right now he may be calling you to do what the disciples did—to wait and devote yourself to prayer until you are endued with power from on high.

E. Stanley Jones often said that "unless the Holy Spirit fills, the human spirit fails."[10] Perhaps some of your recent failures in your efforts to serve Christ have made you painfully aware of that. As never before you realize that without the Holy Spirit, what Christ is calling you to do is mission impossible!

Like the disciples, then, you need to tarry and wait. You need to ask the ascended Christ to send the Holy Spirit upon you, to clothe you with power so you can be his witness and join him in his mission. If so, don't be in a hurry. Devote yourself to prayer. Find others who will pray with you. Search your heart. As you pray, ask Jesus to increase three things in you.

First, ask him to *increase your desire* for more of himself and more of the fullness of the Holy Spirit. "Before we can be filled with the Spirit," said A. W. Tozer, "*the desire to be filled must be all consuming* ... The degree of fullness in any life accords perfectly with the intensity of true desire. We have as much of God as we actually want" (italics mine).[11] In speaking about the Spirit, Jesus himself said, "Let anyone who is *thirsty* come to me" (John 7:37, italics mine). Ask the ascended Christ to make you thirsty by increasing your desire for more of the Holy Spirit.

Second, ask Jesus to *increase your will* to surrender and give up control. Richard Neuhaus was right: "It is our determination to be independent by being in control that makes us unavailable to God."[12] In order to experience more of the Spirit's presence in our lives, we need to surrender areas of our lives in which we are insisting on being "independent by being in control." Where in your life does self need to be dethroned and Christ enthroned? Are there also areas of unhealed hurt and pain where you are holding on to anger, bitterness, and unforgiveness? Ask the ascended Christ, then, to empty you of anything that's preventing the Holy Spirit from being in control. Ask him to increase your will to surrender all to him.

Third, ask Jesus to *increase your faith* in his promise and the heavenly Father's promise to give you the Holy Spirit. Jesus described this promise of the Father's when he said, "If you then, who are evil, know how to give good gifts to your children, how much more will the heavenly Father give the Holy Spirit to those who ask him!" (Luke 11:13). In asking him, then, to fill us with his Holy Spirit, we can be confident that the Father wants to give more than we want to receive. The Father will give the Holy Spirit to those who ask him. We don't have to overcome his stinginess or reluctance to fill us with the Spirit—just take hold of his willingness.

And Christ the Son's willingness too! He himself told the disciples, "It is to your advantage that I go away . . . if I go I will send him [the Holy Spirit] to you" (John 16:7). "And see, I am sending upon you what my Father promised" (Luke 24:49). It is his ascension, as we've already stressed, that has exalted him to the place where he joins the Father in sending the Holy Spirit. As Peter declared in his Pentecost Day sermon, "Being therefore exalted at the right hand of God, and having received from the Father the promise of the Holy Spirit, he has poured out this that you both see and hear" (Acts 2:33).

The heart of the Father longs for you to experience the person, the power, and the presence of the Holy Spirit. And the Son, through his life, death, resurrection, and ascension, has accomplished everything necessary for that to happen. Ask that your faith and confidence in the Father and Son's promise to pour out the Spirit on you will increase. Stand upon their promises.

Devote yourself to prayer, as the disciples did. Ask the ascended Christ to send the Holy Spirit upon you so that you can join him in participating in his mission. Ask him to intensify your desire, deepen your surrender, and increase your faith. Persevere in prayer. Cry out like Jacob did as he wrestled all night with the angel, "I will not let you go, unless you bless me!" (Gen. 32:26). You can be confident that our ascended Lord will bless you if you do. He will give you the Holy Spirit. He will bless you so that, as he fulfills his mission through you, you will truly become a blessing to others.

Questions for Personal and Group Reflection

1. What does fulfilling the Great Commission mean in your life? How have you been called to be on mission for Christ? How would you describe your mission field?

2. How have you been called to be a witness for Christ? Based on Acts 1:8, where is your Jerusalem and Judea (immediate surroundings)? Where is your Samaria (nearby but across cultures) and your "ends of the earth" (all over the globe)?

3. Why is it important to understand the close connection between the ascension and mission?

4. What has been your understanding and experience of the Person of the Holy Spirit?

5. Do you need a fresh outpouring of the Holy Spirit in your life to enable you to fulfill the mission Christ is calling you to?

6. Ask Jesus to (a) intensify your desire, (b) deepen your surrender, and (c) increase your faith in his promise and the Father's promise to fill you with the Spirit. Which of those three do you need to pray most for right now?

Notes

Chapter One: A Mind Set on Heaven

1. C. S. Lewis, *Mere Christianity* (New York: The Macmillan Company, 1960), 118.
2. N. T. Wright, *Surprised by Hope* (New York: HarperCollins, 2008), 111. See also his discussion in *Simply Jesus* (New York: HarperOne, 2011), 195–98.
3. Elizabeth Barrett Browning, "Aurora Leigh," in D. H. S. Nicholson and A. H. E. Lee, eds., *The Oxford Book of Mystical Verse* (Oxford: Clarendon Press, 1917), 86.
4. Maltbie D. Babcock, "This Is My Father's World," *The New Church Hymnal* (Lexicon Music, Inc., 1976), 2.
5. There is some disagreement among biblical scholars about the exact number, ranging from twenty to twenty-three occurrences. I'm following Richard Bauckham, who maintains there are twenty. See his "The Throne of God and the Worship of Jesus" in Carey Newman, James Davila, Gladys Lewis, eds., *The Jewish Roots of Christological Monotheism* (Leiden: Brill, 1999), 43–69. Martin Hengel believes there are twenty-one. See his *Studies in Early Christology* (Edinburgh: T & T Clark, 1995), 133. David M. Hay provides the most exhaustive study and concludes there are twenty-three. See his *Glory at the Right Hand: Psalm 110 in Early Christianity* (Nashville:

Abingdon, 1973). Specific verses that are often cited are Matthew 22:44; Mark 14:62; Luke 22:69; Acts 2:34–35; Romans 8:34; Ephesians 1:20; Colossians 3:1; Hebrews 1:3, 13; 8:1; 10:12; 1 Peter 3:22.

6. See Eugene Peterson, *Christ Plays in a Thousand Places* (Grand Rapids, MI: Eerdmans Publishing Company, 2005), 20–21.

7. See especially Christian Smith, *Soul Searching* (New York: Oxford University Press, 2005); Skye Jethani, *The Divine Commodity* (Grand Rapids, MI: Zondervan, 2009); and Ronald Rolheiser, *The Shattered Lantern* (New York: Crossroad Publishing Company, 2004).

8. Amy Hollingsworth, *The Simple Faith of Mr. Rogers* (Nashville, TN: Thomas Nelson, Inc., 2005), 154.

9. Oswald Chambers, *Prayer: A Holy Occupation* (Grand Rapids, MI: Discovery House, 1992), 82.

10. Gordon Smith, *Called to Be Saints* (Downers Grove, IL: InterVarsity Press, 2014), 53.

11. Charles Wesley, "Jesus to Thee We Fly," *Hymns for Ascension Day* (London: 1789).

12. Andrew Murray, *The Holiest of All* (Tarrytown, NY: Fleming H. Revell, 1978), 65.

13. A. B. Simpson, *The Christ of Forty Days* (Camp Hill, PA: Christian Publications, 1995), 144–45.

14. Charles H. Spurgeon, *Morning by Morning* (Grand Rapids, MI: Baker Book House, 1973), 113.

Chapter Two: The Now and Forever King

1. James Luther Mays, *Psalms* (Louisville, KY: John Knox Press, 1994), 351.

2. N. T. Wright, *How God Became King* (New York: HarperOne, 2012), 16.

3. Richard Bauckham, "The Throne of God and the Worship of Jesus" in Carey Newman, James Davila, Gladys Lewis, eds., *The Jewish Roots of Christological Monotheism* (Leiden: Brill, 1999), 61–62.

4. See his exposition of the Apostles' Creed in Karl Barth, *Dogmatics in Outline* (London: SCM Press, 1949), 124.

5. Kevin Vanhoozer, *Faith Speaking Understanding* (Louisville, KY: Westminster John Knox Press, 2014), 213.

6. Maltbie D. Babcock, "This Is My Father's World," *The New Church Hymnal* (Lexicon Music, Inc., 1976), 2.

7. Brian J. Walsh and Sylvia C. Keesmaat, *Colossians Remixed* (Downers Grove, IL: InterVarsity Press, 2004), 154.

8. Charles Wesley, "Rejoice, the Lord Is King!" *The United Methodist Hymnal* (Nashville, TN: The United Methodist Publishing House, 1989), 715; italics added.

9. Richard H. Mouw, *Uncommon Decency* (Downers Grove, IL: InterVarsity Press, 1992), 146–47.

10. See Luke Timothy Johnson, *Hebrews* (Louisville, KY: Westminster John Knox Press, 2006), 90.

11. Thomas Oden, *Classic Christianity* (New York: HarperCollins, 2009), 494.

12. C. S. Lewis, *The Lion, the Witch and the Wardrobe* (New York: HarperCollins, 2001), 146.

13. George Matheson, "Make Me a Captive, Lord," in the *United Methodist Hymnal* (Nashville, TN: The United Methodist Publishing House, 1989), 421.

14. John Calvin, *Institutes of the Christian Religion,* Vol. I, eds. John T. MacNeil and Ford Lewis Battles (Philadelphia: The Westminster Press, 1960), 497.

15. Ibid., 498.

16. Ibid., 499.
17. James Davison Hunter, *To Change the World* (New York: Oxford University Press, 2010).
18. Richard Bauckham, *The Theology of the Book of Revelation* (New York: Cambridge University Press, 1993), 141–42.
19. T. F. Torrance, *Space, Time and Resurrection* (Grand Rapids, MI: William B. Eerdmans Publishing Co., 1976), 121.
20. Tim Chester and Jonny Woodrow, *The Ascension: Humanity in the Presence of God* (Ross-shire, Scotland: Christian Focus Publications, Ltd., 2013), 43.
21. Richard Neuhaus, *Freedom for Ministry* (Grand Rapids, MI: William B. Eerdmans Publishing, 1992), 71.

Chapter Three: Exalted Humanity

1. See "Excursus: The Son of Man" in Craig Keener, *Acts: An Exegetical Commentary, Vol 2* (Grand Rapids, MI: Baker Academic, 2013), 1437–40. And for an older, though helpful, overall summary, see the chapter "The Son of Man" in George E. Ladd, *A Theology of the New Testament* (Grand Rapids, MI: Williams B. Eerdman's Publishing, 1974), 145–58.
2. Alan Richardson, ed., *A Theological Word Book of the Bible* (New York: Macmillan Co., 1962), 232.
3. Peter Toon, *Heaven and Hell* (Nashville, TN: Thomas Nelson, 1986), 58.
4. Quoted in Robert M. Solomon, *Apprenticed to Jesus* (Singapore: Armour Publishing, 2014), 2.
5. Charles Wesley, "Hark! The Herald Angels Sing," *The United Methodist Hymnal* (Nashville: The United Methodist Publishing House, 1989), 240.

6. Charles Wesley, "Hail, the Day That Sees Him Rise," *Christian Worship* (Exeter: Paternoster Press, 1976), 168.

7. Gerrit Dawson, *Jesus Ascended* (London: T & T Clark International, 2004), 8.

8. Some of this material is adapted from my book *Give Them Christ: Preaching His Incarnation, Crucifixion, Resurrection, Ascension and Return* (Downers Grove, IL: InterVarsity Press, 2012), 143–45.

9. Ibid., 32.

10. Thomas F. Torrance, *Space, Time and Resurrection* (Grand Rapids, MI: William B. Eerdmans Publishing, 1976), 127.

11. Karl Barth, *Church Dogmatics, Vol 4, Part 2* (Edinburgh: T & T Clark, 1985), 153.

12. I am indebted to Anthony Kelly for this term. See his *Upward* (Collegeville, MN: The Liturgical Press, 2014), 49.

13. Peter Atkins, *Ascension Now* (Collegeville, MN: The Liturgical Press, 2001), 71.

14. Dawson, *Jesus Ascended*, 7.

15. Christopher Wordsworth, "See the Conqueror Mounts in Triumph," *Christian Worship* (Exeter: Paternoster Press, 1976), 172.

16. John R. W. Stott, *The Message of 1 Timothy & Titus* (Downers Grove, IL: InterVarsity Press, 1996), 115.

17. Quoted in Leanne Payne, *The Healing Presence* (Grand Rapids, MI: Hamwith Books, 1989), 99.

18. Dietrich Bonhoeffer, *Letters and Papers from Prison* (New York: Macmillan Publishing, 1971), 415.

19. Thomas Merton, *Life and Holiness* (New York: Image Books, 1964), 99–100.

20. Quoted in Solomon, *Apprenticed to Jesus*, 12.

21. Henri Nouwen, *Life of the Beloved* (New York: Crossroad, 1992), 21.

22. Quoted in Leanne Payne, *Restoring the Christian Soul: Overcoming Barriers to Completion in Christ through Healing Prayer* (Wheaton, IL: Crossway Books, 1991), 31.

23. Ibid., 32.

24. See John Cassian (*Conferences* 15.7) cited in Sarah Coakley, *God, Sexuality and the Self* (Cambridge: Cambridge University Press, 2013), 176.

25. Torrance, *Space, Time and Resurrection,* 110–11.

26. Bernard of Clairvaux, *Sermons for the Summer Season,* trans. Beverly Mayne Kienzle (Kalamazoo, MI: Cicercian Publications, 1991), 45–46.

27. Ibid., 36.

28. Ibid.

29. Quoted in Jean LaFrance, *My Vocation Is Love* (Boston: Pauline Books and Media, 2012), 156.

Chapter Four: Always with Us

1. F. B. Meyer, *Daily Meditations* (Westchester, IL: Good News Publishers, n.d.), 12.

2. Thomas F. Torrance, *Space, Time and Resurrection* (Grand Rapids, MI: William B. Eerdmans Publishers, 1976), 132.

3. Some of the material in this section is adapted from my book *Give Them Christ: Preaching His Incarnation, Crucifixion, Resurrection, Ascension, and Return* (Downers Grove, IL: InterVarsity Press, 2012), 144–48.

4. Peter Toon, *The Ascension of Our Lord* (Nashville, TN: Thomas Nelson Publishers, 1984), 5.

5. K. C. Thompson, *Received Up into Glory* (London: Faith Press, 1964), 65.

6. J. G. Davies, *He Ascended into Heaven* (New York: Association Press, 1958), 179.

7. N. T. Wright, *Surprised by Hope* (New York: HarperCollins, 2008), 111.

8. Anthony J. Kelly, *Upward* (Collegeville, MN: Liturgical Press, 2014), 53.

9. Brian Wren, "Christ Is Alive," *The United Methodist Hymnal* (Nashville: United Methodist Publishing House, 1989), 318.

10. Dennis Kinlaw, *This Day with the Master* (Nappannee, IN: Francis Asbury Press, 2002), April 23.

11. Torrance, *Space, Time and Resurrection*, 135.

12. Kinlaw, *This Day with the Master*, March 18.

13. Thomas Chisholm, "Great Is Thy Faithfulness," *The United Methodist Hymnal*, 140.

14. William Dix, "Alleluia, Sing to Jesus," in *Christian Worship* (London: The Paternoster Press, 1976), 208.

15. A. W. Tozer, *The Pursuit of God* (Camp Hill, PA: Christian Publications, 1982), 36–37.

16. See his sermon, "The Means of Grace" in *The Works of John Wesley, 1* (Nashville, TN: Abingdon Press, 1984), 376–97.

17. John Telford, ed., *The Letters of John Wesley, Volume 4* (London: Epworth Press, 1931), 90.

18. Oswald Chambers, *My Utmost for His Highest* (Westwood, NJ: Barbour and Co., 1963), 147.

19. Nicholas Hermann (Brother Lawrence), *The Practice of the Presence of God* (Old Tappan, NJ: Fleming H. Revell Co., 1958), 29.

20. Gregory Boyd, *Present Perfect* (Grand Rapids, MI: Zondervan Publishers, 2010).

21. See Malcolm Muggeridge, *Something Beautiful for God* (London: Collins/Fontana Books, 1972); Leanne Payne, *The Healing Presence* (Westchester, IL: Crossway Books, 1989), 26.

22. Stephen Seamands, *Ministry in the Image of God* (Downers Grove, IL: InterVarsity Press, 2005).

Chapter Five: Power over Our Enemies

1. Charles Wesley, "Rejoice, the Lord Is King," in *Wesley Hymnbook*, ed. Franz Hildebrand (Kansas City, MO: Lillenas Publishing Company, 1963), 97.
2. Charles H. Spurgeon, *The Treasury of David*, abridged by David O. Fuller (Grand Rapids, MI: Kregel Publications, 1976).
3. Jack Hayford, "Majesty, Worship His Majesty," in *The United Methodist Hymnal* (Nashville, TN: The United Methodist Publishing House, 1989), 176.
4. J. R. R. Tokien, *The Fellowship of the Ring* (New York: Houghton Mifflin Company, 1966), 322.
5. Oswald Chambers, *Daily Thoughts for Disciples* (Grand Rapids, MI: Zondervan Publishing Co., 1976), 32.
6. In the discussion of Paul's thorn in the flesh, I have adapted material from my book *Wounds That Heal: Bringing Our Hurts to the Cross* (Downers Grove, IL: InterVarsity Press, 2003), 171–73.
7. Quoted in Paul Barnett, *The Message of 2 Corinthians* (Downers Grove, IL: InterVarsity Press, 1988), 177.
8. "Musings on Augustine's Deepest Wound"; http://vmntblog.com/2015/04/musings-on-augustines-deepest-wound.html. Accessed July 25, 2015.

Chapter Six: An Intercessory Life

1. Some of the material in the following pages is adapted from my book *Give Them Christ* (Downers Grove, IL: InterVarsity Press, 2012), 153–57.

2. Thomas Oden, *Classic Christianity* (New York: HarperCollins Publishers, 2009), 488–89.

3. Charles Wesley, "Arise, My Soul, Arise," in Franz Hildebrandt, ed., *Wesley Hymnbook* (Kansas City, MO: Lillenas Publishing Co., 1973), 84.

4. Charitie Lees Bancroft, "Before the Throne of God Above," in *Christian Worship* (Exeter, UK: The Paternoster Press, 1976), 182.

5. Quoted in Gerrit Dawson, *Jesus Ascended* (London: T & T Clark International, 2004), 133.

6. Quoted in Richard Foster, *Prayer: Finding the Heart's True Home* (San Francisco: HarperCollins Publishers, 1992), 193.

7. Amy Carmichael, *The Gold Cord* (New York: Macmillan, 1932), 31.

8. Charles Wesley, "Arise, My Soul, Arise," *Wesley Hymnbook*, 84.

9. Oswald Chambers, *My Utmost for His Highest* (Westwood, NJ: Barbour and Co., 1963), 258.

10. Douglas Steere, ed., *Spiritual Counsel and Letters of Baron Friedrich von Hügel* (New York: Harper and Row Publishers, 1961), 78.

11. Oswald Chambers, *If Ye Shall Ask* (New York: Dodd, Mead & Co., 1938), 102–3.

12. Charles Wesley, "Soldiers of Christ, Arise," *The United Methodist Hymnal* (Nashville, TN: The United Methodist Publishing House, 1989), 513.

Chapter Seven: Mission Possible

1. Ben Patterson, *God's Prayer Book* (Carol Stream, IL: Tyndale, SaltRiver, 2008), 88.

2. Tim Chester and Jonny Woodrow, *The Ascension: Humanity in the Presence of God* (Ross-shire, Scotland: Christian Focus Publications, 2013), 48.

3. Raymond Brown, *The Gospel According to John, XIII–XXI* (Garden City, NY: Doubleday & Co., Inc., 1970), 1139.

4. G. Campbell Morgan, *The Acts of the Apostles* (New York: Fleming H. Revell Co., 1924), 30–32.

5. Samuel Chadwick, *The Way to Pentecost* (Fort Washington, PA: Christian Literature Crusade, 1969), 15.

6. W. Reginald Ward and Richard P. Heitzenrater, eds., *The Works of John Wesley, Volume 18* (Nashville, TN: Abingdon Press, 1988), 250.

7. W. Reginald Ward and Richard P. Heitzenrater, eds., *The Works of John Wesley, Volume 19* (Nashville, TN: Abingdon Press, 1990), 29.

8. Ibid., 46.

9. John Telford, ed., *The Letters of John Wesley, Vol. 1* (London: Epworth Press, 1931), 286.

10. Quoted in John Akers, John Armstrong, and John Woodbridge, *This We Believe* (Grand Rapids, MI: Zondervan Publishing House, 2000), 147.

11. A. W. Tozer, *The Divine Conquest* (Old Tappan, NJ: Revell, 1950), 124.

12. Richard J. Neuhaus, *Death on a Friday Afternoon* (New York: Basic Books, 2000), 90.